Microcomputer Applications in the Elementary Classroom

A Guide for Teachers

GEORGE W. BRIGHT

ALLYN AND BACON, INC.
Boston   London   Sydney   Toronto

BT afp 12/17/87

Library of Congress Cataloging-in-Publication Data

Bright, George W.
  Microcomputer applications in the elementary classroom.

  Bibliography: p.
  Includes index.
  1. Computer-assisted instruction.   2. Microcomputers.
 3. Education, Elementary—Data processing.   I. Title.
LB1028.5.B676   1987   372.13'9445   86-28715
ISBN 0-205-10454-1

Printed in the United States of America

10 9 8 7 6 5 4 3 2 1 91 90 89 88 87 86

Contents

Preface

There is much excitement about the use of microcomputers in elementary schools. It is precisely now, while parents, school boards, teachers, and students are so excited, that we should begin the long process of thinking deeply about how to integrate microcomputers into the elementary school curriculum. In most schools, microcomputers are an "add-on" to the regular instruction. There is a serious risk that the extra burden this approach involves may turn off both teachers and students to the potential that microcomputers have for improving learning. To counter this risk, we must begin to integrate microcomputers into the regular instructional program of elementary schools.

The topics addressed in this book are, I believe, the most important ones to include in any dialogue on integrating microcomputers into instruction. At the same time, beginning computer users will find the topics accessible; the discussions about instructional uses of computers are centered around learning objectives that are common to most elementary schools. Microcomputers ultimately will be accepted into schools only if learning is improved as a result of their use, so dialogue should focus mainly on the contribution that computers can make to learning.

The primary intended audience for this book is elementary school teachers who have some experience with microcomputers, either through personal use or through watching others use them. No particular expertise is assumed, however. Secondary, but very important, audiences are curriculum and instructional coordinators, workshop leaders, school administrators and planners, and school board members. Each of these groups will find information that may help them plan appropriate uses of microcomputers in elementary schools.

In the best of all possible worlds, this book would be read in the presence of a microcomputer with lots of instructional software. There is no substitute for hands-on experience with a computer. The illustrations in the book can give only a weak impression of the dynamics of using instructional software. Simulations and word processing software are especially difficult to portray accurately through pictures. However, if a computer with lots of software is not regularly available, a few minutes of "play time" on a computer would be very beneficial. Even that limited exposure will help make the concepts come alive.

My bias on the use of computers in elementary schools is that computer-assisted instruction (e.g., drill and practice programs, simulations) will for a long time be a very important application of computers in elementary schools. Over the next decade, use of utility programs (e.g., word processing, data base) will probably come to rival computer-assisted instruction in importance. Utility programs extend our mental abilities, and let both children and adults do old things in different and more efficient ways as well as do new things that would otherwise not be possible. But it will take time to learn how best to stretch children in these directions.

Programming probably will decline in importance for elementary school students in this same period, just as it will decline in importance for adults in the "real" world. Most applications of computers are becoming "friendlier," with less need for the user to know the intricacies of the program that drives the application.

Unlike other educational innovations, computers are in schools partly because parents and students insist that they be. Because of these pressures, computers are not going to be a fad that is here today and gone tomorrow; they are going to remain a part of the teaching environment from now on. Hopefully, this book will help some teachers learn better how to cope and how to use microcomputers effectively to improve the learning of their students.

George W. Bright

Introduction to Computer Education

1

Computer education has become one of the most frequently discussed topics in education today. Its importance lies in the already pervasive and rapidly expanding role that computers play in our everyday lives. Over the past few years pressures have been rapidly mounting from many sources for schools to participate actively in the computerization of society—from parents who want their children to be able to cope with modern technology, from businesses who hire graduates into work environments that are becoming rapidly computerized, from colleges and universities who demand more and more sophisticated skills of high school graduates, and, probably most important, from the students themselves who have become computer-oriented almost as a birthright.

The ways that various schools and school districts have responded to these demands show that there is no clearly articulated policy about computer use in the curriculum. Too often the response has been a rush to acquire equipment without a concurrent careful examination of how that equipment might best be used. On the surface this seems to be analogous to other fads that have previously been enthusiastically embraced by educators. However, on second glance there is an important difference. The impetus for this move is primarily from outside the typical education establishment; pressures are tending to grow rather than diminish, in spite of increased activity by schools to assimilate computers into existing programs.

This book is an attempt to discuss the most important applications of computers in elementary schools so that both preservice and in-service teachers are prepared to discuss the important issues of computer education. It is critical that teachers have substantial input to whatever decisions schools make about the use of computers in schools, for it is the teachers who must ultimately implement any plan of action. Teachers must be at the same time enthusiastic and skeptical about the use of computers. Computer disciples would have us believe that computers alone can solve most of the problems of modern education, while computer skeptics decry computerization as merely another fad that will in time pass. Neither view is accurate; but until teachers have adequate information about the possibilities inherent in computers, they will be unable either to counter these positions or to provide thoughtful alternatives.

UNDERSTANDING THE
COMPUTER AGE

At the outset it is important to have both conceptual and functional understandings of a computer. Conceptually a computer is an electronic device (e.g., a "black box") that can accept, manipulate, and communicate information. One analogy is that of a learner; a learner accepts information through reading or listening or watching, manipulates that information by relating it to other information s/he knows and storing it in long-term memory, and then communicates that information through exams or discussions or behavior. One major flaw in this analogy, however, is that we know very little about the process of manipulation of information in the learner's mind. In a computer the manipulation is through a computer program that can be studied in detail by anyone who wants to find out how the manipulation is being done.

A computer might also be viewed as a fancy calculator, for a calculator performs all of the same functions. Again, however, the analogy tends to break down because a computer has capabilities that a calculator cannot encompass. The information that is given to a computer can be in the form of numbers or text or in electronic pulses from game paddles, light pens, or a variety of other fancy devices. It is expected that soon many computers will even be able to accept voice input; the user will only have to talk to the machine. The output of information from a computer can also take almost all of these forms. The same computers that recognize voice input will almost certainly also have voice production capabilities, so the machine will be able to talk to the user as well as display information on a monitor screen.

The types of manipulations inside a computer are almost unlimited; the imagination of the programmer is the only real restriction. Too, the speed of manipulation is far greater than that of a calculator. In large computers several million operations per second can be performed, and even in microcomputers several thousand operations per second are common. The memory available in a computer is also much larger than in a calculator, oftentimes the equivalent of hundreds of thousands of characters. Perfect recall of such vast quantities of information gives computers a distinct advantage over many humans.

Functional understanding of a computer only comes through hands-on use. Of course, a computer can be used for programming; but probably equally important, it can be used as a tool to do such things as word processing, keeping records, and searching a data base for particular information. Obviously the printed book cannot provide hands-on experience; the reader will have to acquire that elsewhere. Access to a computer would be an excellent accompaniment to reading this book. However, this book illustrates information displays that are generated by these kinds of uses. These illustrations will give some feel for computer uses.

WHY ARE COMPUTERS IMPORTANT?

Computers are important primarily because they extend the intellectual capabilities of humans. First, computers can perform repetitive tasks (e.g., print form letters or payroll checks by the thousands) more accurately and with much less expense, both monetarily and in personal exhaustion, than humans. This capability extends humans' abilities to deal with the world; indeed, the existence of large institutions, like schools, businesses, or cities, often requires that many people get similar, but nonetheless individualized, information. Computers can help provide this information.

Second, computers can remember and manipulate enormous quantities of information. This capability expands both the quantity and the accuracy of memory in humans and potentially makes decisions better. Some futurists have estimated that by the end of the century the amount of information in the world will double about every one and one-half years. This means that by the time an entering first-grader leaves grade six, the amount of information in the world will be sixteen times as great as when s/he began school, and by the time s/he graduates from high school, the amount of knowledge in the world will be 256 times as great as when s/he entered first grade! There is no hope for mere humans to be able to keep up! Computers will help by enabling people to locate information relevant to a particular question. Computers will do the "leg work" to narrow the field of vision on a given topic.

Third, as more is learned about how people make decisions and about how to write computer programs to model those decision-making processes, computers will be able, and almost certainly allowed, to make some decisions. This will relieve humans from some of the tedium of their lives and will allow them to concentrate on more important decisions. For example, in the summer of 1984 a computer made a decision to abort a U.S. space shuttle mission; this decision was made only four seconds prior to lift-off. The computer actually shut down the rocket engines without even asking the human controllers. Certainly one reason the computer was given this power is that the computer can receive information about a malfunction, process that information, and make a decision about how to act on that information in only a split second—far faster than a human could. But probably equally important is that the computer always interprets the information in the same way; there is never any idiosyncratic bias.

Different humans might interpret the importance of a malfunction differently because they were tired or angry or depressed. When lives are at stake, such as in a space mission, it is comforting to know that important decisions can at least partially be regulated by unbiased and consistent decision processes.

There is a belief that computers are suddenly appearing all around us in new applications. That is not true. What is true is that with the increase in miniaturization of computer technology people are suddenly aware of the many uses of computers. Computers are already part of automobiles and most major appliances that are now manufactured. With advances in voice recognition and synthesization, people will be able to talk to these machines and get answers from them. For example, when a car is started, it will be able to perform diagnostics on its systems and tell the driver when one of the major systems, like the brakes, needs to be fixed.

The trend toward the infusion of computers into more aspects of our lives is not likely to end soon. Simply coping with the world—for example, the information explosion—will require an ever expanding role for computers. As a consequence, it may become less important for students to learn specific content than to learn how to deal with information. That means that exposure to computer capabilities and limitations is vital for every educated citizen. The schools must play a primary role in providing this exposure, and this means in turn that teachers must acquire that knowledge as soon as possible. This book will help some begin that journey.

Birnbaum (1985) notes that computer use is in the third of four evolutionary stages for technologies: (a) experimental rarity, (b) exotic tool or toy, (c) quantity manufacturing, but used by only a small part of the population, and (d) absence more noticeable than presence. Further, more and more people are now focusing on the development of human resources through computers rather than on the cost of obtaining the needed computer power. This signals the entry to the fourth stage. Concurrently, software will need to be created that extends people's capabilities instead of trying to make people fit software's limitations. Building computer use into the schools in ways that are consistent with the fourth stage is the biggest educational challenge today.

WHY ARE COMPUTERS IMPORTANT IN THE CLASSROOM?

As with most innovations in education, there has been much speculation about whether computers will soon take over the jobs of teachers. Certainly they will not, though the roles that teachers play will change somewhat.

During the late 1960s, when computer-assisted instruction was first being implemented on large mainframe computer systems, it was predicted that teachers would become an endangered species. Claims were made that computers could perform most of the teachers' functions better and ultimately for less cost. That prediction was far off the mark; in fact, neither part of it has proven to be the case. Some low-level, repetitive tasks like drill and practice can certainly be performed better and cheaper by computers, but the overall job of a teacher cannot. Now most educators have recognized that the appropriate concern is to identify the parts of teaching that can best be performed by computers.

Mitzel (1981) focused on one of these roles: computers can and should help educators adapt instruction to each learner. Five ways he listed to do this are to provide instruction (a) at a self-determined pace, (b) at times convenient to the learner, (c) at a point when prerequisites are in place, (d) by first diagnosing and then remediating the learner's difficulties, and (e) with multiple media (pp. 94–95). Each of these ways can be incorporated into computer-delivered instruction, but only with intentional effort.

A second role is to teach new concepts with computer technology that could not be taught without it. One such concept is computer programming; no one can adequately learn to program without hands-on experience with a computer. Another such concept is database searching; the time required to search multiple data bases by hand is becoming prohibitive.

Probably equally important is identifying changes in the standard curriculum that will be required as computers are incorporated into the teaching of everything from art to zoology. Some reorganization of traditional curriculum practices is inevitable in order to take advantage of the capabilities of the new technology. For example, in social studies the concepts that are likely to survive computerization are those that help people organize and interpret information. Identifying historical precedents is likely to be far more useful to people than remembering details about historical events. Such general concepts have always been important, of course, but in many ways their application depended on remembering information that could be used as the raw material for generating a statement of historical precedent. Now the computer can be used as the memory device for this information, and people can focus on asking the right questions of the machine to get the relevant information out of that memory.

COMPUTER LITERACY

One of the reasons that computers are being introduced in so many elementary school classrooms is so that the schools can begin to provide the conceptual and functional understanding of computers to students. This typically goes under the rubric of computer literacy, though that term can have many different definitions. It is often impossible for schools to adopt a definition that will satisfy all of the external pressure groups, and indeed it is often because of outside pressure that a computer literacy curriculum is developed. Parents, business persons, or indeed the students themselves may believe that without such a curriculum a school is automatically deficient.

Although computer literacy is an important topic for schools to consider, one of the goals of this book is to put that topic into an overall perspective on computer education. Computer literacy is not the only important thing that computers can be used for in schools; it should share with other priorities the often-scarce computer facilities that are available. It is also likely to be important for only a relatively brief time, say a few years, until most teachers become equipped to deal with computers in the context of teaching other content.

Computer literacy is important for students primarily because of their need to deal with computerization in everyday life. So many aspects of life will involve the use of computers that it will soon become impossible to understand fully what is going on without some familiarity with computers. Schools, while they should not be expected to make experts out of their students, should be expected to provide exposure to the relevant concepts.

TYPES OF COMPUTER-ASSISTED INSTRUCTION

One of the first encounters that many people have with computers is through commercially prepared software. Instructional software of this kind is referred to as computer-assisted instruction (CAI), and it may be of several types.

Drill and practice CAI is the computer analogy to worksheets. Exercises of one type are provided repeatedly so that the learner can gain adequate practice to overlearn the content. Usually after each response the learner is given feedback on the correctness of that response. This type of CAI is relatively easy to write, and consequently most of the early commercial packages were in this mode. The primary advantage over noncomputer worksheets is that feedback is provided after each response, so a student does not repeatedly practice an incorrect procedure before learning that it is incorrect. Drill and practice CAI, however, does not take advantage of many of the unique capabilities of the computer.

Tutorial CAI is analogous to teacher presentation of material, either for a whole class or a small group. Tutorials are usually difficult to program, since they must account for a wide variety of student responses to every question. Early in the learning of new content, students often seem to have acquired bizarre variations of what was intended to be taught. Tutorial CAI must seem to be as intelligent as a teacher in responding to and correcting those incorrect first impressions.

Simulation CAI models simplified versions of real-world events. Their primary use is to allow students to make decisions about those events without having to live with the perhaps disastrous consequences of those decisions. These are roughly analogous to role-playing in noncomputer settings; students can pretend to be heads of corporations, leaders of nations, managers of wildlife reserves, or even elements in a chemical reaction.

CAI games overlap all of these categories, for any of them could be cast in the context of a game. The most common type of instructional CAI game is drill and practice game; this is like regular drill and practice, except that feedback is typically not explicitly provided for each response that the student makes. Rather, success at winning the game becomes the criterion of understanding of the content. Tutorials or simulations can also be cast as games, though it sometimes becomes difficult to know how well winning actually reflects understanding of the content rather than understanding of how to win. Sometimes the strategies for winning such a game are not well grounded in the content intended to be the taught.

All types of CAI have analogies in noncomputer classroom instruction. Transfer of a particular instructional technique to computer format, however, does not carry with it a guarantee that the computer version will be equally effective. There are many unanswered questions about the ways that students interact both with computers and with the information presented on a monitor screen. Until careful research is completed to begin to answer these questions, teachers should be skeptical about claims of the effectiveness of CAI, especially when those claims are based on the noncomputer versions of similar techniques.

TEACHING PROGRAMMING IN ELEMENTARY SCHOOL

As mentioned earlier, one of the obvious things that can be taught with computers is programming. But just because it can be taught does not mean it should be, especially in elementary school. As a school begins to develop a definition for computer literacy, it is almost automatic that programming be discussed; and indeed, understanding adequately the capabilities and limitations of computers seems to be easier after some experience in programming. Consequently, it is probably important and appropriate for all students and teachers to have a chance to learn some programming skills. But determining the amount of exposure to programming is difficult.

Programming can be taught as a foreign language (after all, it has a grammar and syntax all its own), and experience has shown that young students learn a foreign language easier than older students. Thus, initial exposure to programming might best come during the elementary school years. However, the goals for such instruction should be relatively limited. Certainly, there should be no expectation of making students into sophisticated programmers.

The choice of programming environment is also probably critical for the success of such instruction. One very desirable goal is to help students develop an understanding of algorithms and of problem solving through breaking a big problem into smaller chunks. A language such as Logo is designed to facilitate this process as much as possible, while a language such as BASIC is not so easily bent to this goal. As with any instruction, the technique must match the goal in order for the instruction to be effective.

OTHER USES OF COMPUTERS

There are many other ways that teachers can use computers to improve teaching effectiveness. Computers can keep records, print out worksheets and tests, help write reports through spreadsheet programs and word-processing programs, and manage students in continuous progress programs. These functions are related to, but are distinct from, the CAI uses discussed earlier. Those who are putting pressure on educators to bring computers into the schools might not see the importance of these applications, for they often seem not to have immediate consequences for instruction in the classroom. However, they may prove to be some of the most important educational applications; it is through these that teachers will develop a sensitivity for computerization in the world around us. Passing on this sensitivity to students may be the best public service that teachers can perform.

Before schools or parents rush into purchase of microcomputers for use by elementary school students, they should consider the concerns and recommendations of Chaffee (1982).

1. One computer in a school generally does not produce a significant experience for students.

2. Without adequate training of teachers in computer use, students will not learn the potential of computers.
3. Students who have access to computers at home generally become more expert than teachers who have no computer experience.
4. Determining both immediate and future goals for computer use in a school may take as long as a year. In all cases, it takes longer than expected.
5. Many questions need to be considered:
   a. What are the purposes of computer use in the school?
   b. Who will monitor the instruction on computer use?
   c. Who will identify software to be used? How will current information on software be acquired and maintained?
   d. How will evaluation of software and of the effectiveness of software be done?
   e. How will teacher education be supported?
   f. Who will be in charge of equipment?
   g. Where will equipment be housed? What kind of security will be used?
   h. Who will schedule use of equipment and resolve conflicts in its use?
   i. Is the electrical system of the school capable of supporting computer equipment throughout the building?
   j. How will repairs be handled? (pp. 17, 76)

Focusing on these concerns will increase the likelihood of a successful implementation of computer use in any school. Laying the proper foundation for computer use is vital to avoid unrealistic expectations by teachers, parents, and students.

AS YOU READ ON

Please keep in mind that this book was written to provide a context for computer education. None of the topics is covered to exhaustion, and many questions will be left unanswered. Indeed many questions are at this time unanswerable. It is primarily through our collective experience with the use of computers in the schools that we will begin even to imagine what the answers might be. Hopefully, however, this book will provide a sound foundation for further learning.

Drill and
Practice Programs

2

Historically many of the objectives of instruction in elementary school have centered on skill and concept learning which requires drill and practice for mastery. Although there is a trend toward expansion of those objectives to include goals like problem solving, there will certainly continue to be a need for students to engage in drill and practice activities. Virtually all such activities can be adapted to computer-assisted instruction (CAI) as one of the primary modes of presentation.

WHAT IS DRILL AND PRACTICE CAI?

The term "drill and practice" refers to any situation in which the same kind of exercise or problem is presented repeatedly and for which students are typically expected to provide a single correct response. For example, students might be asked to write the plural of each word in a list of nouns, to match musical pitches, or to estimate the product of two two-digit numbers. In the last example, there may be a range of answers that can be considered correct, but usually there is only one correct answer for each exercise.

    One of the standard ways to provide drill and practice is through worksheets, which might be prepared by the teacher for a particular purpose or which might be provided along with a curriculum program. One significant disadvantage of worksheets is that the student may complete an entire set of exercises incorrectly and rehearse incorrect procedures repeatedly before any feedback is provided by the teacher (or an answer key) on the accuracy or inaccuracy of those procedures. Incorrect procedures, if they are rehearsed with the belief that they are correct, may become embedded so deeply in cognition that it becomes extremely difficult to unlearn them and to relearn correct procedures.

Drill and practice CAI goes a long way toward alleviating this deficiency. It can provide immediate feedback after each exercise to indicate whether the result of the student's procedure is correct. Students thus are given clues about the accuracy of their procedures. These are, however, *only clues* about the procedures. The feedback is an evaluation of the answers, not necessarily of the processes used to obtain those answers.

Beyond this very simple use of the computer's capabilities, drill and practice CAI can also include diagnosis of a student's difficulties, can provide remediation for those difficulties, and can select for extra practice those exercises that cause particular difficulty for an individual student. More will be said in Chapter 6 about diagnosis. For now, it only needs to be pointed out that remediation can then be tailored to fit the difficulty, or combination of difficulties, that a particular student is experiencing.

The capacity to select for extra repetition the exercises that are causing difficulty is one that probably has not received enough attention by authors of drill and practice CAI. A program can easily keep track of how many times each exercise is answered correctly or incorrectly. Each incorrect response could increase the probability that this exercise will be presented again. For example, in a drill and practice program on multiplication basic facts, the sevens and eights facts typically cause the most difficulty. However, for some children the zero facts are also frequently answered incorrectly, apparently due to confusion with addition facts. A drill and practice program can identify those particular facts that an individual student is having difficulty with and present those facts more frequently. Keeping records for each child individually means that the time spent on skills that are already mastered is kept to a minimum. A worksheet approach to drill and practice must repeat the facts that children collectively miss rather than only those facts that a particular individual is having difficulty with. Collective repetition will be inefficient for some of the students.

CONTENT OF DRILL AND PRACTICE CAI

Drill and practice CAI programs should deal only with exercises that can be responded to quickly and with little work required away from the computer. For example, a CAI drill and practice program on two-digit by three-digit multiplication would be inappropriate if only the final product were to be typed in at the keyboard. Considerable work on paper would be required before the answer could be typed in, so the computer would spend most of its time sitting idle and waiting for the student to compute the product. Although there might be an advantage in having the computer diagnose errors in such a complicated skill as this, CAI programs that drill subskills would be a considerably more efficient use of available computers than drill on the full skill.

Complex skills, however, can be incorporated into drill and practice CAI through the use of the computer as a tool for completing some parts of the skill. For example, multiplication of decimal fractions could be practiced by having the program display an exercise along with the product of the two factors as if there were no decimal point in either one. The student could then be asked to identify where the decimal point should be placed. At the point in the curriculum in which this skill is practiced, textbooks frequently assume that multiplication of whole numbers is not going to be a difficulty. Rather the placement of the decimal point is more frequently the focus of attention. Whether this assumption is correct varies from class to class, but the use of the computer to perform the multiplication puts the emphasis on the new material to be learned. Follow-up exercises could be employed to determine if more practice is needed with multiplication of whole numbers.

BAD AND GOOD FEATURES OF
DRILL AND PRACTICE CAI

The most frequent deficiency with drill and practice CAI is that too many extraneous gimmicks are employed. For example, the feedback for a correct response may be a "smiley face" drawn on the screen or a tune played for several seconds. As one-time feedback devices, these are undoubtedly very effective; but as devices to be used tens of times with each student, they become quite distracting and time-consuming. Too, they may hold the child's attention during the use of the program and inhibit attention from being focused on the content to be learned.

Another undesirable feature of drill and practice CAI programs is that wrong answers sometimes produce more elaborate feedback than correct responses. For example, in some versions of Hangman the graphics display for the "hanged" man is more interesting to students than the simple "correct" response presented for spelling the word correctly. Many children intentionally misspell words just so that they can see the fancy graphics.

Even a simple noise that is given as feedback for responses can be quite disconcerting even if the program is used by only a few students at a time in the back of the room. That noise can cause disruption of other activities that are going on in the classroom, and other students may not be able to concentrate on those activities. At the very least every program should give the teacher the option of turning the sound off.

Many of the commercial drill and practice programs also involve gamelike situations that expose children to imaginary violence that would not be used in a standard worksheet situation. For example, there might be an alligator eating fish or a space creature shooting at monsters. Whether repeated exposure to these situations causes any long-term effects on the ways in which children perceive the world around them is not known. However, the possibility certainly exists, and at the very least schools should probably get a feeling from parents of whether the fantasy situations provided in such drill and practice programs are acceptable.

Good features of drill and practice CAI programs include the use of a variety of feedback responses for both correct and incorrect answers. For example, short positive phrases could be randomly selected by the program for use after each correct response. After an incorrect answer the student should have an opportunity to respond again, as the first response may have merely been mistyped. The number of tries allowed before the correct answer (or corrective remediation) is given is an instructional decision made by the program designer. It is related to the kind of content involved, the age of the intended audience, and the importance of the content to the elementary school program. The designer's decision may not be the same as a particular classroom teacher's preference, and the congruence between these two outlooks may be critical in the decision of whether to use a particular program in a particular elementary school setting.

Another desirable feature of drill and practice CAI is a large pool of exercises from which particular ones are selected. If the pool is too small, students may begin to recognize particular exercises and to remember the answers to those exercises. This obviously defeats the purpose of drill and practice, except for specialized areas in which there really are only a few possible exercises to practice.

There are many commercial examples of drill and practice CAI. In fact, much of the current educational software could be classed as drill and practice CAI. As with text material, the quality of this software is quite variable. Most of it does not take advantage of the positive things that microcomputers can do to enhance learning. Rather, most software could be described as electronic worksheets whose only advantage is in providing immediate feedback for each response.

DRILL AND PRACTICE IN PRIMARY GRADES

Drill and practice CAI in the primary grades should probably be used only in small doses, spread over an extended period of time. Although students seem to be very motivated by the use of microcomputers in the classroom, these machines have not been in use long enough for anyone to know what the saturation level is. That is, how soon will these same students grow tired of the new technology? And equipment is generally still scarce, so short sessions with drill and practice CAI will help give access to these resources to as many students as possible. It is undoubtedly unrealistic to expect that classroom sets of microcomputers will soon be available as standard equipment in an elementary school classroom.

Drill and practice CAI should not be used to replace other instruction; drill and practice in any of its forms cannot, and is not expected to, do that. But this type of CAI can put some variety in the repertoire of techniques that a teacher has available to use. Such variety may even enhance the effectiveness of standard drill and practice activities, just because they will not be used as frequently and will have the advantage of novelty.

Two very important characteristics of drill and practice CAI for primary grades are appropriate reading levels and simple input procedures. A program to drill writing the past tense of verbs cannot be used if the instructions for the program use vocabulary that even a sixth-grader would not understand. Because primary-grade children cannot be expected to have well-developed keyboard skills, a program should accept inputs with only a few keystrokes (preferably only one).

Some examples of appropriate content for drill and practice programs for primary-grade students are color recognition, word-numeral associations, arithmetic basic facts, simple grammar skills, shape names, plurals, and rhyming words. Every response should receive some simple feedback, and reinforcement should be given at the conclusion of the program.

Some sample screens from a drill and practice program on addition facts are given in Figure 2.1 (MECC, 1983). (Please keep in mind, both here and for later illustrations, that no printed document can quite capture the full impact of the visual images provided by CAI. Some imagination is required from the reader in order to visualize the "flow" of information from one screen to the next.) Reinforcement is given through drawing parts of an airplane in response to correct answers. The exercises ask not only for missing sums, such as in screen 3, but also for missing addends, such as in screens 2 and 4.

The best advice on drill and practice CAI for primary grades is, "Keep it simple!" Use this CAI to provide some variety in instruction, but don't expect too much from it. Other uses of computers (for example, teaching programming) should not be squeezed out to make

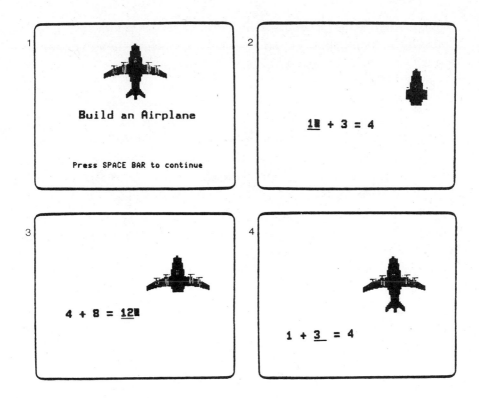

Figure 2.1   Arithmetic drill screens
From MECC, *Early Addition*, page 12.

room for drill and practice CAI. This CAI is only one of the appropriate uses that can and should be made of microcomputers in the primary grades.

DRILL AND PRACTICE IN INTERMEDIATE GRADES

More complex skills can be drilled in the intermediate grades. The feedback provided after each exercise, however, should still be kept simple. Summary feedback (for example, the percentage of correct responses) can be provided at the end of each session, and students can be asked to keep personal records of their progress. Intermediate-grade students can be assumed to have, or can develop, better key-board skills than primary-grade students. Less care, though certainly some care, must be given to keep the instructions and the input procedures simple.

This CAI can be used to provide relearning or review for students who have been absent, to provide extra practice for students who haven't yet learned a particular skill, or for some simple remediation for students who are having difficulty learning a skill. All students, however, should be given opportunities to use this CAI; students should not perceive this drill as just for the "dummies."

Figure 2.2 shows screen displays from a language arts program (MECC, 1980a). In this program students are to practice use of pre-fixes. The cycle of events is simple: an exercise is presented, the response from the student is accepted, and feedback is provided. The exercises range over checking for meaning of a prefix, writing a word containing that prefix, and using the prefix in context. At the end of the program, summary information is provided. Figure 2.3 shows screen displays from a review lesson for five prefixes. At the end of this review, summary information is again provided.

Any program with only the capabilities of this one would be especially useful for students who are having repeated difficulty with prefixes. It is too simple for anyone who has essentially mastered the skill, though it would relieve the teacher from having to monitor the practice of a student. Drill and practice programs should provide summary information both to the student and to the teacher about the success rate of the user. Without this information the teacher would have to rely on additional testing to determine whether the student had adequately learned the material.

Figure 2.4 provides displays for a program with similar goals for learning; that is, memorization of particular facts (MECC, 1980b). This program drills the state names and the state capital names. Of particular note about this program is its use of graphics. Instead of relying on only textual presentations, it gives a visual display that is more powerful. For example, in this way the state name could be asked before the capital name.

Two kinds of memorization are required for success with this program. First, the student must pair the state name with the picture

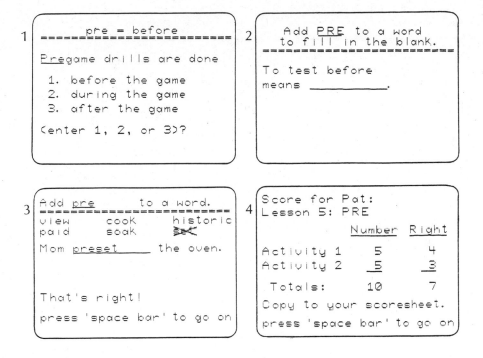

Figure 2.2 Language arts drill screens

From MECC, *Elementary*, Volume 5, pages 34, 35.

Add un,re,dis,pre or in
================================
                fill
The ship's crew must
_____ the fuel tank
after the flight.

Lesson 7:

	Number	Right
Activity 1	13	11
	—	—
Totals:	13	11

Copy to your scoresheet.
press 'space bar' to go on

Figure 2.3 Language arts review and summary findings screens

From MECC, *Elementary*, Volume 5, pages 45–46.

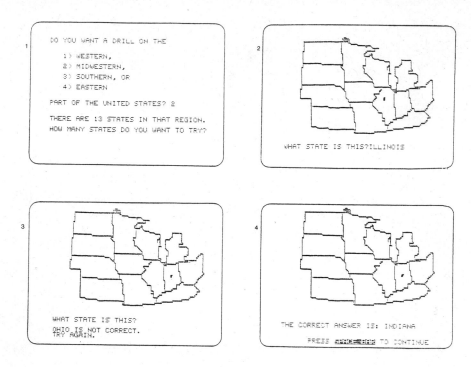

Figure 2.4   Geography drill

From MECC, *Social Studies*, Volume 2, pages 93–94.

of that state. Second, the name of the capital of the state must be paired with the name of the state. The multiple modes of representation of information (pictures and words) may use both hemispheres of the brain, and success with the two modes may be different. It should not be expected that students who are successful with the first kind will necessarily be successful with the second kind. Recognizing differences like this will become increasingly important for teachers who use software that employs more modes of representation of information (e.g., pictures, text, sound) than can be presented in text material.

Feedback in drill and practice programs does not have to be merely right or wrong. In some programs a score is kept, with the number of points awarded for correct answers differing according to the form of the answer. In dealing with common fractions, for example, more points could be given if the answer is reduced to lowest terms than if the answer is correct but not reduced. In this way positive feedback is given for every correct answer (a very desirable trait), but the reward is greater for use of a more efficient form.

RESEARCH ON DRILL AND PRACTICE CAI

Much of the research that has been done on CAI has dealt with drill and practice programs. Most frequently, the results have been that students learn about the same amount of material through CAI as through conventional instruction but that this learning is achieved cither in less time or at a faster rate with CAI (e.g., Bracey, 1982; Cody, 1973; Edwards, Norton, Taylor, Weiss, and Van Dusseldorp, 1975; Jamison, Suppes, and Wells, 1974; Kulik, Kulik, and Cohen, 1980; Overton, 1981; Thomas, 1979).

The studies in which this result has been observed span elementary school through college and cover content as diverse as mathematics, typewriting, and identification of handicapped students. Most of the studies, however, have been conducted with secondary school students and with science-oriented content, though newer research tends to be conducted with younger students. Most of the studies have also dealt with fairly large pieces of content, such as a whole unit, rather than with a particular skill, such as writing plurals of nouns. Again, recent research is more frequently addressing smaller skills. Jensen (1982), for example, used microcomputers to teach addition facts to first- through third-grade students. He reported that time savings occurred and suggested that this was because of careful repetition only of the problems that were causing difficulty.

The observation of roughly equivalent learning in less time has been referred to as the "CAI phenomenon" (Bright, 1983) and may offer one of the primary advantages of drill and practice CAI in the classroom. If the same learning can be accomplished through CAI in less time, then the time saved can be spent learning new material or learning the same material to a deeper level of understanding. In either case, the productivity of the classroom teacher would be improved, and the knowledge base of the students would be greater.

The two most probable explanations for this phenomenon arise from the results of the Beginning Teacher Evaluation Study conducted in California in the 1970s. The subjects for that study were second-graders and fifth-graders, and achievement was examined in both reading and mathematics. One of the strongest predictors of student achievement was the amount of time a teacher was able to keep students on task with activities that they could perform successfully. This time was labeled "academic learning time."

CAI may increase the amount of academic learning time in two ways. First, computer technology is a strong motivator and tends to keep children focused on the screen display; that is, focused on the content. Second, by taking advantage of the computer's capability to keep track of a student's performance on exercises, those exercises that are being missed consistently can be identified, and remediation (or at least informative feedback) can be provided. This remediation may prevent the wrong processes from being learned, with the result that students spend less time practicing wrong processes. They are more apt to spend more time practicing correct processes, thus increasing the academic learning time.

In the area of affective outcomes the research is quite a bit less clear. Bracey (1982) in his summary of the CAI literature points out that students seem to come out of CAI use with better attitudes about computers, they seem to enjoy the ability to determine the pace at which they move through material, and they generally feel more in control of things during CAI. These outcomes are probably all viewed as desirable by most elementary school teachers.

Fisher (1984) in another survey of research also reported that students feel more positive about both themselves and school as a result of computer use, though the studies on which this conclusion was based seem to be mostly with college students. He also reported indications of attendance increases and vandalism decreases, at least partially as a result of computer use in schools. He also reported (a) that there is more social interaction among groups working at computers, (b) that three students per terminal is adequate but that four is too many, causing some students to wait for a turn and to waste time, (c) that teachers with access to computers spent more time with individual students than teachers without computers, and (d) that girls are underrepresented in computing classes, at all grades but especially at higher grades. He noted that anecdotal reports, though consistent, are not sufficient to clearly establish believable results in the area of social effects of computers. Controlled studies are needed to confirm results.

In summary, research clearly indicates that CAI should not be expected to produce miracles. It must not be oversold. The learning produced could be good or bad, just as with any instructional technique, depending on the care with which the designer constructs the program. Too, CAI should not be used to the total exclusion of other techniques. No technique alone can long succeed in teaching everything, and there is not yet enough information about the long-term effects of CAI on learning to know how it can best be used. In particular, no one knows if the apparent motivating effect will wear off after repeated exposure. At the moment CAI appears to be a very promising technique, but, like the development of instructional television, program designers must become more sophisticated as the learners become more used to using CAI.

CONCLUSION

As long as drill and practice is necessary for attaining the goals of elementary school education, drill and practice CAI will have a role to play in providing that instruction. The research clearly indicates that there is at least one advantage of CAI over other modes of drill and practice; namely, time can be saved. Teachers, however, must demand that drill and practice software take full advantage of the capabilities of the computer without cluttering the instruction with inappropriate uses of those capabilities. As with any instructional material, care must be taken in the selection of the particular software that is used to be sure that it teaches objectives that are important and that it will be an efficient use of students' time.

Tutorial Programs 3

In the elementary school new information is most often presented to students by the classroom teacher. Typically, the teacher tells the students something, or demonstrates something, and the students are supposed to remember or model what the teacher has done. Much of this information is presented to whole classes at once, and then a great deal of time is spent in helping those students who did not grasp the new material the first time it was presented. Tutorial programs may be effective either in presenting material for the first time or in helping teachers do the reteaching.

WHAT IS TUTORIAL CAI?

A tutorial CAI program is any program that teaches new information to the user. In addition, most tutorial programs also check on the user's level of understanding, and many tutorials provide some drill and practice of that material. However, the key aspect of tutorial programs is their intent to teach new material. For example, a student might be presented with rules for writing plurals of one-syllable words, with plans for designing electric circuits, or with an algorithm for multiplying common fractions. If the intent is to teach this material as if it were previously unlearned, these programs would be considered tutorial programs.

In self-contained classrooms most of this kind of information is presented by the teacher, with practice and additional explanation provided by a textbook or workbooks. For a wide variety of reasons not all students grasp a new concept with the first explanation. For example, students may lack the necessary prerequisite skills, they may be daydreaming, they may be ill or hungry, they may be uninterested, they may misunderstand the words that the teacher uses, or they may be absent. It is often difficult for the teacher to know, and impossible for printed materials to find out, how well the instruction has communicated its intended content. That is, what level of understanding have the students attained? Microcomputer tutorial programs can overcome this deficiency by analyzing responses of each student during the course of the instruction. All of the responses can also be remembered with full accuracy, so each student's history is complete.

Typically, a tutorial program performs this analysis by asking questions during the presentation and matching the responses with common wrong answers that are stored in the program. In this way the program can sometimes identify for the students the incorrect aspects of their understanding and provide an alternate explanation of the material to try to correct that misunderstanding. For example, if a student responds with "runed" for the past tense of "run," the program might respond with "The past tense of many verbs can be formed by adding an -ed, but *run* is a special verb. The ordinary rules for forming the past tense do not apply. The correct past tense is *ran*." In this way the student is given some positive feedback about knowing the general rule, but the limits of that rule are further defined, and perhaps with this information the student will be more successful later. Providing feedback at this point in the learning process may also reduce the amount of reteaching that will be needed later because misunderstandings are corrected before they become too firmly established in memory.

Most tutorial programs analyze responses simply by matching the students' answers with possible wrong answers stored in the program by the program author. A teacher with experience in teaching a given topic, on the other hand, often has both a large set of typical wrong answers that students give to specific questions and associated notions of what misconceptions those answers may illustrate. Such notions are, of course, only guesses in any particular instance, and at best they reflect general kinds of misunderstandings. Any particular student may have acquired some unusual misconception that has behavioral manifestations similar to a common error, so the teacher's attempt at remediation may be off target. A tutorial program would analyze students errors unbiasedly and might be more likely to identify uncommon errors.

As tutorial programs become technically more sophisticated, they will employ better techniques for diagnosing misunderstandings (see Chapter 6). With a better diagnosis comes a better explanation of the error, and the program is more likely to change the students' understandings from incorrect to correct.

THE STRUCTURE OF A TUTORIAL PROGRAM

A tutorial program has a simple generic structure; each new concept or skill is presented in three basic steps. Information is presented, a check is made on how well the student understood that information, and corrective action is taken if necessary so that the student's understanding is the same as that intended by the author of the program. The creativity needed for writing an effective tutorial program is usually not in writing the initial teaching presentation. Rather it is, first, in designing appropriate questions to find the most critical misunderstandings and, second, in creating effective reteaching sequences for correcting those misunderstandings. Most reteaching sequences will never be seen by most users; only a few will ever be encountered by any individual. However, without these sequences, the tutorial program would fail in one of its most important characteristics; namely, correcting misconceptions that a particular individual may develop during instruction.

Misunderstandings may develop for a variety of reasons; for example, lack of necessary prerequisite information or misunderstanding of the language used in teaching. Keeping track of even a few of these creates a tutorial program with very many branching possibilities. As a consequence, a tutorial program will typically be very large, perhaps too large to be stored in the working memory of most types of microcomputers. In this case pieces of the program will have to be stored externally—for example, on a disk. Thus, tutorial programs usually have more hardware requirements (for example, disk drive required) than drill and practice programs. If tutorial programs are to be an important part of the use of microcomputers in a school, adequate hardware will need to be purchased. This may be an important cost in the use of tutorial programs in schools.

In teaching the addition algorithm, for example, students may make a variety of errors, some of which are listed below. (The problem, $57 + 78$, is used as the example, with expected wrong answers given in parentheses.)

1. drops carry digit (25 or 125)
2. carries wrong digit (711 or 171)
3. begins on left (117 or 216 or 261)
4. adds each column separately (1215)

Some students will exhibit several of these errors in succession, while other students may exhibit only one error and that one only briefly. A tutorial program must always be alert for all errors. Unlike a human, who comes to expect certain types of errors from specific students and who may not recognize other errors, a tutorial program can recognize errors without bias or predisposition.

This objectivity has both advantages and disadvantages. The primary advantage is that the program can recognize changes in a student's behavior almost as soon as it occurs. There is no lag such as might be caused by the human tendency to see only what is expected or desired. The primary disadvantage is that time may be lost in repeatedly searching through an entire list of potential errors trying to find the error(s) that fit.

USES OF A TUTORIAL PROGRAM

There are two obvious uses of tutorial programs. One is to provide the primary instruction on a topic. Another is to provide backup instruction for students who were absent, or did not grasp the material, during the first exposure.

The first use may bring to mind an image of a mythical twenty-first-century school (and myth is probably the proper analogy) in which every student has a computer and spends most of the day interacting with that machine. Even though this view is not accurate, there will likely be some time spent each school day in human-machine interaction. Tutorials will take up a significant portion of that time. Much of this tutorial use will likely be for teaching material of which the teacher is unsure or that has special presentation requirements, such as the need for accurate pictures or animation. Tutorials are not likely to replace teachers as the primary source of new information, but in some areas tutorials can supplement the information that a particular teacher has. For example, the calls in the mid-1980s for more science education in the U.S. may be met more easily and inexpensively with the development of adequate microcomputer tutorials than with the massive in-service and preservice education required to educate all, or even most, elementary school teachers.

The second use of tutorials would relieve one burden for teachers; namely, repeating instruction for students who were absent or who weren't paying attention during the initial instruction. Teachers could then focus their energies more effectively on correcting those misconceptions that are not corrected by the tutorial. After all, no tutorial can be totally effective for all students; teachers will always be needed to fill in the gaps in the program.

WHAT CONTENT IS APPROPRIATE FOR TUTORIALS?

Tutorial programs should deal with content that involves rules or relationships. Simple memorization of isolated facts would be the domain of drill and practice more than of tutorials. Content that is best presented with illustrations, either static or with motion, is particularly appropriate, since pictures can be easily and cheaply manipulated on a monitor screen.

Science concepts seem especially appropriate for tutorials since they typically are built on prerequisite material, involve many relationships, and can frequently be presented through pictures. A microcomputer tutorial program can determine whether the prerequisite material is mastered (and either provide additional instruction or send the student to the teacher for extra help), can identify and isolate the relationships between parts of the material, can present extra explanation to help develop understanding of those relationships, and can employ color and motion in various combinations to correct misunderstandings.

For example, Bork (1981, 1983) has developed tutorial programs for teaching science concepts for a variety of ages and situations. The early programs were for college-age students, with whole courses provided in CAI mode (on mainframe computers rather than microcomputers). More recently, however, he has developed microcomputer programs for use in unattended environments, like libraries, where people of all ages and many diverse backgrounds simply walk up and start using the programs. Much analysis of responses is required in these programs, since they can make no assumptions about the previous experiences of the users. Some of these specific programs include electricity (connecting a battery to turn on a light) and simple genetics. The teaching technique used is "to place students in an environment in which they must behave like scientists in their approach to problems" (1983, p. 50). This technique is reminiscent of the science curriculum projects of the 1960s and hopes to communicate the flavor of science rather that its full content.

Programs like these would seem to be especially useful in elementary school for topics in which teachers are generally not expert. The background of the classroom teacher may not be much more extensive than that of some students, and computer programs designed to identify and correct misconceptions may be much more effective just because the teacher may not recognize the misconceptions of students or may not be able to correct such misconceptions efficiently.

TUTORIALS IN THE PRIMARY GRADES

In the primary grades tutorials might be used as an alternate mode of instruction to help students focus on simple concepts and relation-

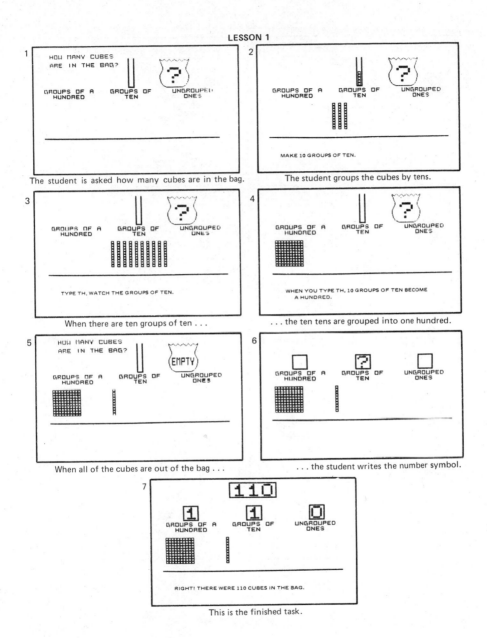

Figure 3.1　Arithmetic tutorial: First lesson

From NCTM, *1984 Yearbook*, page 46.

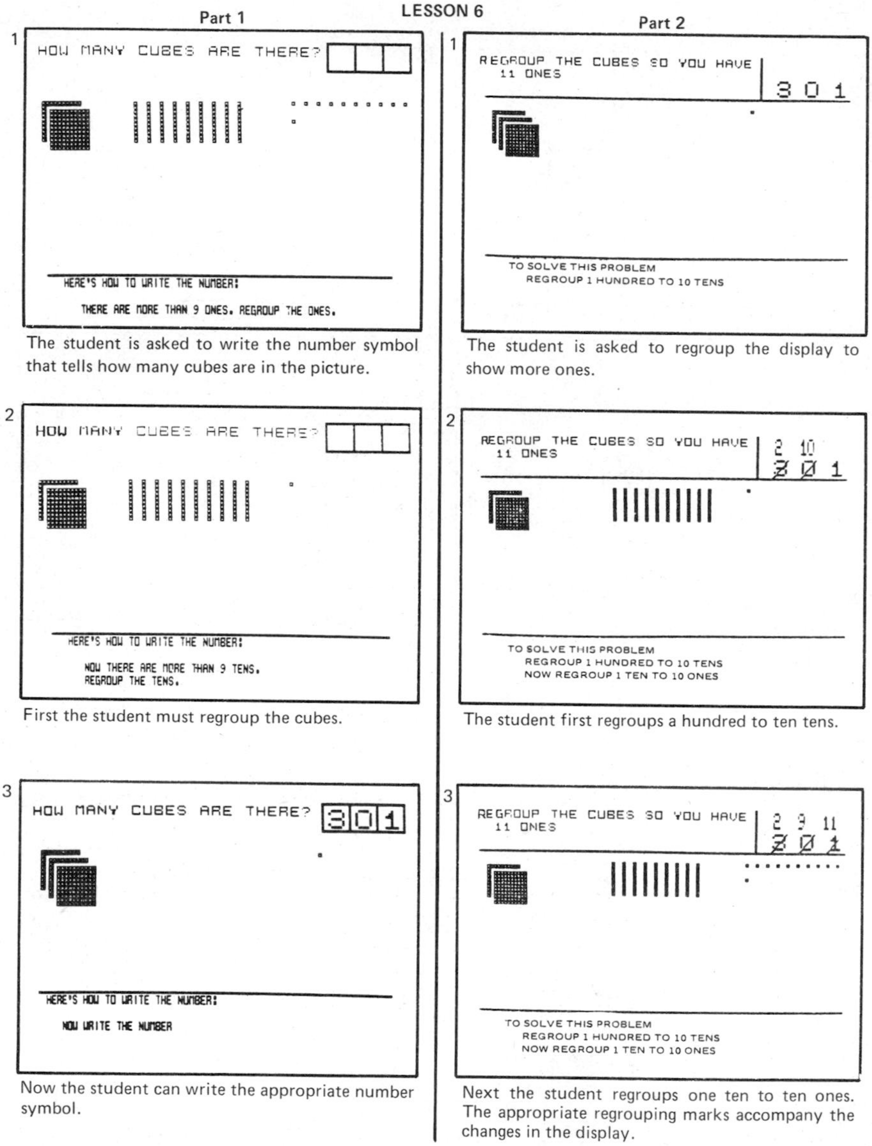

Part 1:

1. The student is asked to write the number symbol that tells how many cubes are in the picture.
2. First the student must regroup the cubes.
3. Now the student can write the appropriate number symbol.

Part 2:

1. The student is asked to regroup the display to show more ones.
2. The student first regroups a hundred to ten tens.
3. Next the student regroups one ten to ten ones. The appropriate regrouping marks accompany the changes in the display.

Figure 3.2 Lesson to link symbols to objects

From NCTM, *1984 Yearbook*, page 48.

ships. Students in these grades are operating at the concrete operations level, so relationships among concepts (and relational concepts) will be difficult to learn. Ordinary whole-group instruction in these areas is likely to fail to take account of the many different misconceptions that students develop because of their limited abilities to process information. Computer tutorials are more likely to help individual students acquire concepts that will not need to be unlearned later.

One suitable tutorial program for primary grades is shown in Figures 3.1 and 3.2 (Champagne and Rogalska-Saz, 1984). The tutorial is designed to help students connect numeration concepts embodied in manipulative materials with the symbols used to write large numbers. A lot of interaction is required from the user, but it is of a different quality than drill and practice programs require. The user must stay involved with the content in order to progress through the program.

TUTORIALS IN THE
INTERMEDIATE GRADES

In the intermediate grades tutorials can deal with more sophisticated content. One such program is Lines (MECC, 1980a), shown in Figure 3.3. This program presents information (screens 1 and 2) and then checks for understanding (screens 3 and 4). This is more typical of most commercial tutorials than is the previous example.

The program also has accompanying print materials that support the instruction on the screen. These include recording sheets on which students can copy some of the definitions and illustrations from the screen and worksheets for further practice.

Another tutorial program is Fish Circulation (MECC, 1980b) shown in Figure 3.4. This tutorial is designed to teach the circulation system of fish. Graphics are used extensively both as a model of the circulation system and as a highlighting device to focus attention on parts of the model. Again, there are extensive print support materials.

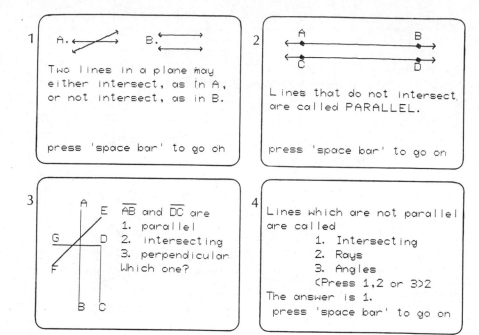

Figure 3.3 Tutorial on lines

From MECC, *Elementary*, Volume 9, pages 10, 14.

Figure 3.4 Science tutorial

From MECC, *Science*, Volume 3, pages 8–9.

BAD AND GOOD FEATURES OF
TUTORIAL PROGRAMS

The current difficulty with many microcomputer tutorial programs is that they do not provide enough branches for the learners. The new information may be presented in only one way, and the only procedure for correcting misunderstandings is to use the same presentation again. This is not much different than the teacher who says the same thing louder when a student asks a question. Also, too much information is often given in text form rather than in other modes of representation. The tutorial program becomes too much of a page-turning device.

Tutorials that were written in the middle and late 1960s for mainframe computers generally provided much better instructional sequences, at least in terms of branching, than current microcomputer versions. At least in part this is due to the fact that early tutorials were only in text mode (because of the limitation of the equipment to teletype terminals) and were written almost exclusively for college students rather than elementary school students. The kinds of reteaching through text explanations that can be done for this older population are more sophisticated because of the accessibility to language.

At the elementary school level considerable creativity is probably required to create reteaching sequences. Effective tutorials will likely be slow to develop until better procedures are available for pinpointing precisely the misunderstandings that students' responses indicate. Too, more needs to be known about the use of pictures, motion, and color in developing understanding. Currently, tutorial authors are effectively limited to authoring by intuition; the research base is too sparse. Until microcomputers became generally available, there was no technology, except people, that could support tutorial teaching. Now the technology exists; instructional strategies must catch up.

This concern about how understanding develops points out the need for research on learning and teaching. Drill and practice is fairly well understood; paper and pencil is an adequate technology to support drill and practice. It is clear to all teachers that drill and practice assists the acquisition of skills. However, at the level of concepts, very little is commonly known about how to make teaching more effective. The advent of the use of microcomputers in the schools will put pressure on software producers to create tutorials for use in schools. Effective tutorials would more likely be produced, however, if more were known about how people learn concepts and relationships among concepts. This knowledge can only come about through research on learning, but it may be the pressures (and the money) of commercial producers of software rather than the search for knowledge that push researchers to develop that knowledge. An analogy can be found in the development of technology for the manned space flight to the moon. It was not until the commitment was made to put a human on the moon that the research was conducted to allow the creation of the technology. The same may be true of accumulation of knowledge about learning, the impetus being more commercial than academic.

EVALUATING TUTORIAL PROGRAMS

Teachers need to look at many different features of tutorial programs in deciding which ones to use in the classroom. Of primary importance are the accuracy of the content presented and the consistency of the pedagogy used with that of the teacher. Since tutorials can be expected to be integrated into the regular instruction, and not to replace that instruction, the philosophy of the tutorial should be consistent with that of the classroom teacher. At the same time, however, the goal of a tutorial program is to instruct, so the information communicated must be accurate.

The nature of the interaction is also very important in tutorial programs. There should be ample opportunity for the students to respond to questions, yet the program should not be just drill and practice. Too, a program that only provides information in screen after screen of text is not a tutorial. There must be interaction between the program and the student. A rule of thumb is that if more than three or four screensful of information are presented without any chance for interaction, there is not sufficient interaction. However, the kinds of questions are equally important. If all of the questions are cognitively at a low level, then the program may just teach memorization of information. For most kinds of content, this level is inadequate. There should be some questions that require careful understanding and analysis of the content.

Also, the questions should not all be multiple choice. Students should have to type in some answers in free response form. This means in turn that the program must be able to analyze such responses and look for key words, even if they are not spelled quite correctly. For example, in a program on flow of blood through the body, one question might be, "Through what does blood flow away from the heart?" Responses of "artery," "the artery," "artary," "artory," "arteries," and variations of these should all be considered correct. Creating programs that can search free responses for a variety of answers is conceptually not difficult, but taking the time and the care to do so makes the production of such programs expensive.

The most difficult part of evaluating tutorial programs for potential classroom use is that it takes quite a lot of time to do the evaluating. Teachers must try out many of the paths that students might encounter. That means that teachers must pretend to make both the common and the uncommon mistakes that students are likely to make in answering the questions. Since it is not possible either to "speed read" through the program or usually to retrace one's path through the tutorial, the teacher must run the tutorial program several times in order to find out what the program can and will do. Although tutorial programs have many advantages, and although schools may find the prospect of using tutorials very attractive, the expense in time of reviewing the programs may discourage teachers, and many school administrators, from making much use of such programs.

WHAT DOES RESEARCH SAY ABOUT TUTORIALS?

There is very little research on the use of tutorial programs with elementary school students. Most of the tutorial programs have been written for college-age or high-school-age students, and much of the research on these programs was conducted with text-only tutorials written for mainframe computers with teletype terminals only. Hence, the conclusions cited below should be viewed rather skeptically. The generalizations to younger populations who are much less verbal can only be tentative.

It is perhaps significant that Overton (1981) in a review of the research on CAI in mathematics discussed no studies of tutorials for elementary school students, and she only referenced the work on PLATO with elementary school students. (The PLATO system is a mainframe computer equipped with multiple terminals.) These PLATO studies (e.g., Slattow, 1977) showed that of the three mathematics-content areas of fractions, whole numbers, and graphs, only the tutorials on fractions resulted in significantly improved learning, as compared to a control group. A similar but less controlled experiment on language arts did not indicate any significant improvement in measures of learning.

In short, tutorials with elementary school students have had no spectacular success in improving learning. However, the development of tutorials is in its infancy; appropriate supporting technology is only now available. As more tutorials are written, and as more research is conducted on those tutorials, more success will certainly be demonstrated. Until that time, teachers should expect tutorials to teach as well as, but certainly no better than, ordinary instruction. Tutorials should be used only if a particular program seems to fit easily into the regular curriculum.

CONCLUSION

Tutorials open up many possibilities for improving the delivery of instruction. As yet, however, these are untried possibilities. It is an exciting time to be studying instruction, but progress is likely to be slow. The science of teaching and learning has not yet established enough principles to guide rapid development of tutorial programs.

Games 4

The idea of using games as teaching devices is quite old. It is widely accepted that ancient civilizations used games to teach, or at least practice, many physical skills. It is not equally accepted, however, that games can teach common educational objectives, even though most elementary school teachers have adapted or created games to try to teach something to their students. The development of computer technology and the accompanying video-arcade technology has given new impetus to trying to understand both how games teach and what kinds of concepts and skills can be taught through games.

WHAT IS A GAME?

Many authors have given many different definitions of a game. Bright, Harvey, and Wheeler (1985) have tried to characterize a game rather than to completely define it. Their list of characteristics is the means for identifying a game in this chapter.

1. A game is freely engaged in.
2. A game is a challenge against a task or an opponent.
3. A game is governed by a definite set of rules that describe all of the procedures for playing the game. In particular, the goal(s) sought are set forth in the rules, and after a play is made, it may not be retracted or altered.

4. Psychologically, a game is an arbitrary situation clearly delimited in time and space from real-life activity.
5. Socially, the events of a game are considered in and of themselves to be of minimal importance.
6. A game has a finite number of states or positions; that is, only a finite number of different things can happen. The exact states of the game are not known prior to the start of the game.
7. A game ends after a finite number of plays.

These criteria are designed to capture the common notions (a) that the rules of a game completely determine it, and if the rules are changed the game has likewise changed, (b) that the game is not completely like real life, and (c) that the game is of minimal long-range importance, even though the skills needed to play the game may be quite important. Yet, because the game is a challenge, there is motivation to play seriously. Players do not simply make random moves, unless they have become completely frustrated.

An instructional game is a game for which the teacher has determined a set of instructional objectives prior to the time at which the game is given to students to play. It is important in choosing a game for instructional use to consider what the instructional objectives of the game are. If instructional objectives for a particular game are not clear, that game should probably not be considered an instructional game, and it should probably not be included in a teacher's instructional repertoire.

Microcomputer games must meet this same test of instructional quality before they are given to students to play. Typically, video-arcade games are not instructional games, for they have no clear instructional objectives. Some people have argued that eye-hand coordination is one outcome of arcade games, but since that is not a typical instructional objective of most elementary schools, the argument becomes quite weak in justifying the inclusion of arcade games in the elementary school curriculum.

VARIETIES OF GAMES

Games can be classified in many ways. Bright et al. (1985) have used two different classifications of games. One is based on the timing of the game relative to the regular instruction designed to produce mastery of content, and the other is based on the cognitive level of the content being taught.

A game can be used either as review or practice of content already mastered (i.e., at the post-instructional level), or as part of the primary instruction designed to produce mastery of the content (i.e., at the co-instructional level), or as readiness for instruction designed to produce mastery of the content (i.e., at the pre-instructional level). Post-instructional games are stereotypical of games in elementary school. That is, most people think games are useful only in drill and practice settings after the primary instruction on a topic. However, there is no logical reason why games cannot also be effective in co-instructional and pre-instructional settings. Recent research on the use of games has shown that games can teach content effectively in a variety of settings, though clearly not every game will automatically do so. At the moment, it is not clear what characteristics or level of content of games may make them effective in different settings.

The second classification is based on Bloom's taxonomy (1956) of educational objectives. There are six levels: knowledge, comprehension, application, analysis, synthesis, and evaluation. In the elementary school setting the first three have always been important, though the next two are becoming increasingly important, given the new emphasis on problem solving. Again, recent research indicates that games can be effective at most of these levels of content, but there is no guarantee of success for any particular game.

Another classification of games has been given by Dennis, Muiznieks, and Stewart (1979). They identify free-form games, rigid-form games, and open-form games. Free-form games can also be called simulation games, and they are characterized by a scenario in which the play progresses (p. 2) and in which the players take on roles. More will be said about simulation games in Chapter 5. Rigid-form games are the typical content-related games that are used in classroom instruction. These kinds of games are discussed below. Open-form games are essentially problem-solving situations that have very little if any relevance to real-world situations. An example of such a game is chess. It is not at all clear, though it is certainly possible, that becoming good at playing chess teaches anything either that will transfer to non-chess situations or that is important to common educational objectives.

Any particular choice of categories of games (called a taxonomy) is arbitrary. The primary purpose of such taxonomies is to help identify the uses of a new game by grouping it with other similar games whose uses are known. In this way the analysis of a new game can be shortened and time can be saved.

WHAT CAN GAMES TEACH?

Games by their very nature provide repetition of situations with slightly different constraints; for example, different numbers rolled on a pair of dice. Hence, games can best teach concepts and skills that need to be encountered repeatedly for mastery. This does not mean, however, that only drill and practice settings are appropriate for game use. It is possible for a game to provide all of the instruction on new content merely through the repeated exposure to situations in which that content is used.

Conversely, games should not be expected to teach content that is encountered only a few times or that requires extensive discussion by a group of people to investigate. For example, unusual problem solving could not be taught by a game, simply because the repeated exposure to problems of the same type violates the necessary requirement that the problems be unusual or novel. Certainly the subskills needed to solve novel problems could be taught through games, but the putting together of those subskills could not be taught through game playing.

CREATION OF
MICROCOMPUTER GAMES

Most microcomputer games are designed to reflect many of the motivating attributes of arcade games. That is, microcomputer games make use of fancy graphics and fantasy situations. Although such "extras" are not an essential part of a game, these features seem to make playing the games more enjoyable.

The critical concern of a teacher, however, should be that the instructional objectives of the game be clear and effectively tied into the play of the game. For example, the game, Flashcard Baseball, does not have the content tied into the play of the game. Students answer questions only in order to allow them to "run" around the bases and to score points. The kinds of questions asked can be changed arbitrarily without altering the rules of the game. If a student is not caught up in the fantasy of the baseball situation, it would be unreasonable to expect this game to teach content very effectively. On the other hand, the game, Teasers by Tobbs (O'Brien, 1982), is quite dependent on the content involved. If that content were changed, say to geometry or to language arts, the game would have to change dramatically. For this reason Teasers by Tobbs is probably a more effective instructional game than Flashcard Baseball, in the sense that the players become more involved with the content being taught. There are fewer distractions away from the content, and learning the content becomes critical for completing a turn in the game.

Also of concern in microcomputer games involving graphics and fantasy is the appropriateness of the fantasy in the context of the goals of the school. For example, many mathematics drill games for elementary school students involve some violence in the fantasy situation; for instance, shooting down spaceships. While this fantasy may be attractive to some students, it may actually be counterproductive for others. Malone (1980), for example, reported evidence that suggests that males may like this kind of fantasy more than females. Such differences among populations of students need to be taken into account in selecting games for classroom use.

GAMES IN THE PRIMARY GRADES

In the primary grades games can teach recognition of color and shape, vocabulary, number facts, and other fundamental concepts. Students enjoy playing games and will often spend great amounts of time playing them. The games should not be too competitive, however, since winning may become important at the expense of learning the content.

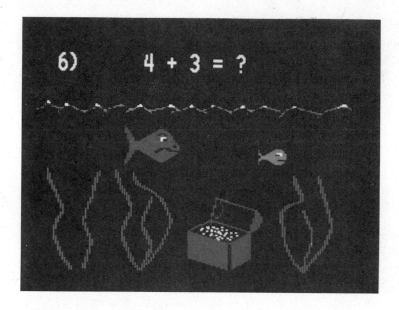

Figure 4.1   Fish Chase

From NCTM, *1984 Yearbook*, page 55. Reprinted by permission of Milliken Publishing Company, St. Louis, Missouri.

One effective game is Fish Chase (Kraus, 1982a). This, like many microcomputer games, is a speed drill, in this case on arithmetic basic facts. The user's choice of fast or slow speed increases the range of students that could make use of this game.

Another game for this level is Jar Game (Kraus, 1982c). This is a pre-instructional game that is designed to give students some intuitive experience with probability. Students choose one of two jars from which squares of two colors are then randomly selected. Students get points when gold squares are chosen, and they get bonus points for choosing the jar with the greater ratio of gold to nongold squares.

GAMES IN THE INTERMEDIATE GRADES

In the intermediate grades games can provide problem-solving experiences and analysis skills in addition to continued instruction on

Figure 4.2 Jar Game

Reprinted by permission of Milliken Publishing Company, St. Louis, Missouri.

fundamental concepts and skills. Teasers by Tobbs, for example, provides experiences with addition and multiplication facts at several
levels of Bloom's taxonomy.

In the first screen display only basic facts are needed to fill in the
blank space indicated by a question mark. However, in the second
display the student must develop a string of deductions in order to
fill in the space indicated. This is one kind of reasoning that is useful
in many problem-solving situations.

Four Letter Words (Luster, 1983) could be made into a competitive
game by using it in a tournament setting, with students' scores determining their rankings. A four-letter word or combination is chosen
by either the user or the computer. Using these four letters, perhaps
with repeated use of letters, students make as many four-letter words
as possible. The program checks each word against those in its accompanying dictionary of over three thousand words. The score is the
total number of words made. After the student finishes, the computer
prints on the screen all of the words in its dictionary that could have
been made.

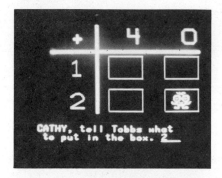

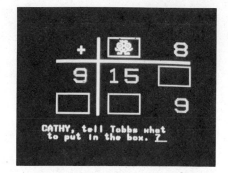

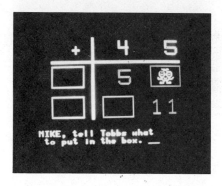

Figure 4.3   Screen displays of Teasers by Tobbs

Used by permission, Sunburst Communications, Inc.

Golf Classic (Kraus, 1982b) is designed to improve estimation of length and angle measurements. After a student chooses the angle and length of a shot, the program draws the path of the shot. The student thus gets immediate visual feedback on the accuracy of the estimates.

RESEARCH ON GAMES

Almost no literature on the effects of microcomputer games exists. There is, however, quite a lot of literature on noncomputer games. It is reasonable to expect most of the results of this work to be gener-

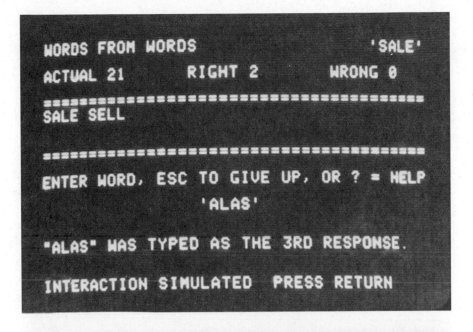

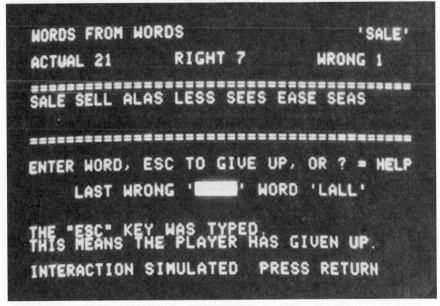

Figure 4.4 Screen displays from Four Letter Words

Written by Robert G. Luster. Published by CONDUIT, The University of Iowa, Oakdale Campus, Iowa City, Iowa.

```
WORDS FROM WORDS                               'SALE'
ACTUAL 21            RIGHT 7            WRONG 1

SALE SELL ALAS LESS SEES EASE SEAS ALAE
ALEE EELS ELLS ELSE LASE LASS LEAL LEAS
LEES SALS SASS SEAL SEEL

SCORE 7              GRADE 33%              TRY HARDER
G = GO ON            M = MENU              ? = HELP


MENU WAS CHOSEN WITH "M"
INTERACTION SIMULATED  PRESS RETURN
```

Figure 4.4   *(continued)*

alizable to microcomputer settings, for it is probably the instructional intent of a game that is important rather than the particular format of that game. The only caveat to generalizing in this way is the unknown influence of the use of graphics and fantasy on the effects that have been observed. Most noncomputer games do not make significant use of these characteristics.

The learning effects and the affective effects of studies with elementary school students will be considered separately. The learning effects will be grouped according to the instructional levels (pre-instructional, co-instructional, and post-instructional) of the games used. For two reasons, the studies cited deal only with mathematics content. First, much more research has apparently been conducted in mathematics than in any other content area; second, the range of content in these studies is quite large. Thus, the results from this literature are fairly representative of the kinds of results that can be expected from games.

Games used at the pre-instructional level have spanned a wide

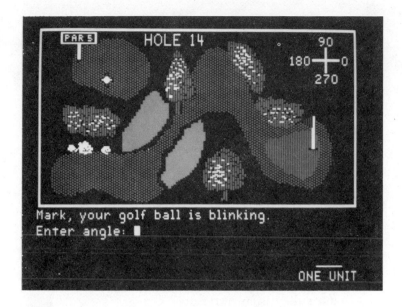

Figure 4.5 Golf Classic

From NCTM, *1984 Yearbook*, page 58. Reprinted by permission of Milliken Publishing Company, St. Louis, Missouri.

variety of content, some of it quite unusual for the elementary grades. Lesh and Johnson (1976) used games to teach motion geometry to 240 fourth-graders. They concluded that the nongame treatment for teaching this content was more effective than the game treatment. Bowen (1970) also compared a game treatment with a nongame treatment to teach logical principles to fourth-graders. He concluded that the nongame treatment was more effective. Trimmer (1978), on the other hand, concluded that with third- and fifth-graders, the game, Mastermind, can be effective at improving reasoning skills. Bright, Harvey, and Wheeler (1983) used the same game with sixth-graders and found no significant improvement in logical reasoning skills. Peele (1972) tried to teach strategy skills to fifth-graders through a variety of games, but he found no significant differences between the game players and the nongame players.

Number skills and arithmetic seem like much more ordinary content than logical reasoning and strategy skills. Humphrey (1966) used games to teach number skills prior to instruction by the classroom teacher. He found no significant effect of the games. Droter (cited by Ashlock and Humphrey, 1976) extended this work to kindergarten students, but again there were no significant results. Wheeler and Wheeler (1940) used a flashcard, bingo-type game to teach number recognition to first-graders, and although statistical tests were not used, they concluded that the game had considerable value for primary children. Karlin (1972) designed a game to teach prime factorization and recognition of the fundamental theorem of arithmetic to fifth-graders. Only recognition of the fundamental theorem of arithmetic improved through game playing. Bright, Harvey, and Wheeler (1980a) did successfully teach probability to older elementry school students in a pre-instructional setting, and other studies with older students (e.g., Goldberg, 1980) have also been successful. Perhaps the development of cognitive abilities that apparently comes with age and experience accounts for the different results.

At the pre-instructional level, then, games have proven successful with elementary school children in only limited settings. This is not too surprising, however, since a pre-instructional game may require that students have enough content background to benefit from it. Many elementary school students simply may not know enough to profit from pre-instructional games.

At the co-instructional level, studies with elementary school students seem to have been more effective. Steinway (1918) in a very early study used number games along with regular instruction in first-grade classrooms. The group that played only games improved more than the group that played games along with regular instruction. Hoover (1921) used games that stressed number operations in third-grade classes. The games group improved more than the regular instruction group, though because the experiment spanned several months, other instruction may have confounded the results.

Ross (1970) taught number concepts successfully to primary-age, educable mentally retarded children, and Wynroth (1970) taught the natural number system successfully to first-graders. Wolff (1974), on the other hand, compared a competitive game, a cooperative game, and a worksheet treatment with first- and second-graders, but he found no significant differences. Fishell (1975) tried to teach division to fifth-graders through game playing, but he, too, found no significant differences when compared to a regular instruction control group.

In spite of the somewhat mixed results, the majority of co-instructional studies have reported either that the games treatment was an equally effective teaching device or that the games treatment was significantly better than the nongames treatment. It is noteworthy that these studies seem to deal almost exclusively with number skills.

The most universally positive results have been observed at the post-instructional level. Bright, Harvey, and Wheeler (1979a) taught multiplication and division basic facts to fourth-, fifth-, and sixth-graders at the start of the school year. The games used were effective at retraining the students' skills. In a longer-term study (Bright, Harvey, and Wheeler, 1980b) the same games were used throughout the school year to maintain skills. Again, the games were effective teaching devices, even as the length of time between game-playing sessions increased.

Attempts to affect students' achievement by increasing the amount of verbalization by students during game playing (Bright, Harvey, and Wheeler, 1980c) were not successful with third-, fourth-, fifth-, and sixth-graders. Similarly, the use of extra manipulative materials with a game of ordering common fractions (Bright, Harvey, and Wheeler, 1981) did not improve the effectiveness of the game, though all com-binations of materials and the game were effective at teaching or-dering of fractions.

Kraus (1981) used the microcomputer game, Fish Chase, to teach addition facts and the microcomputer game, Hangman, to teach spell-ing to second-graders. The arithmetic game was effective, but the spelling game was not.

In summary, the post-instructional games have been generally successful, though attempts to improve on those effects (e.g., Bright, Harvey, and Wheeler, 1979b) have not been very successful. Virtually all of the games have been of relatively low-level content, and this fact makes it difficult to compare these results with results at other instructional levels.

In a major study of affective outcomes of games Malone (1980) concluded that computer games are motivating because (a) there is a clearly identified goal, (b) attainment of the goal is uncertain, though possible, and (c) achieving the goal, or at least making progress toward achieving the goal, tends to increase self-esteem. Further, many computer games are embedded in a fantasy; some fantasies are extrinsic to the game content (e.g., Flashcard Baseball), while others are intrinsic (e.g., legislature simulation). Intrinsic fantasies seem to be more interesting and more instructional. Fantasies involving emotion (e.g., shooting down aliens) are likely to be more popular than less emotionally laden fantasies; however, Malone's data indicate that among elementary school students preference for various fantasies differs according to gender. Boys, for example, liked the popping balloons in one version of a darts game, while girls disliked it. A range of fantasies is thus necessary in a school's collection of computer games.

CONCLUSION

Microcomputer games seem to be a good use of computer capabilities. The computer can check to be sure that students play by the rules and answer any content questions correctly. Students enjoy playing these games, and they are likely to spend considerably more time engaged with the content in this form than in many other instructional forms. The research on effects of games also suggests that games can be effective if used judiciously. Teachers should feel encouraged to use microcomputer games and to expect learning to result.

Simulations   5

Simulations may become the most important type of instructional computer program by the end of the century. A computer simulation typically takes advantage of more of the capabilities of computers— e.g., graphics, rapid data processing, branching according to user inputs—than other types of CAI. As the capabilities of microcomputers increase, more and more complex simulations will be possible. It may even be possible to teach some kinds of content through a simulation (for example, complex relationships) that would be impossible to teach in any other way.

A computer simulation is a program in which a few features of a real-world situation are abstracted and then are used to form a model of a simplified version of that same situation. The model is based on only the few abstracted features, so by its very nature it is different from the real-world situation that inspired it. In a simulation the user either watches the modeling process, if it is completely self-contained and driven by the program, or participates in it by providing values for some of the variables that are specified in the program. Typically, a computer simulation either speeds up a process, as in a legislature simulation, or slows down a process, as in a chemical reaction simulation, so that the user can watch each step along the way within the time constraints of a normal classroom environment.

Although noncomputer simulations have been available for many years, it is not uncommon to discover that an author's instructional objectives for a simulation are somewhat vague. Probably the most important objective of a simulation is to illustrate the relationships between the variables chosen for inclusion. That is, how do the variables interact? At the same time, measuring understanding of relationships is difficult at best, and that may account for the lack of important learning effects attributable to the use of simulations in the classroom. However, the truth may be that researchers simply have not been looking in the right places for learning outcomes.

UNIQUENESS OF SIMULATIONS AS CAI

There are several differences between a simulation program and the drill and practice or tutorial programs discussed in earlier chapters. First, a simulation typically involves more complex material. A drill and practice program is usually narrowly focused on one skill or concept, and a tutorial also has a primary objective of communicating content. Irrelevant side trips in a tutorial tend to distract the user from that objective. Simulations, however, focus on interactions between conditions or variables, each of which has more than one value. The large number of possible combinations of these values automatically guarantees that understanding the simulation is going to be a complex process.

Second, a simulation is usually not completely self-contained; that is, the user is responsible for control of some of the features of a simulation. Drill and practice programs and tutorial programs, because they have narrow content foci, must assume the major responsibility for sequencing material for the user. Simulations are written to respond to any user inputs, within predetermined acceptable limits, and to model the effects of those inputs on the real-world situation under consideration. The user can experiment with the simplified situation by providing combinations of the variables that the program author might not have explicitly anticipated. At the very least, because of the large number of possible combinations, some users will choose combinations that the author did not test during trial runs; there are too many combinations for all of them to have been tried.

Third, the instructional intent of most simulations is to communicate information or understanding of the processes that are part of the situation being modeled. That is, the instructional intent is one of the aspects of problem solving. This means that a single simulation might be used for a variety of instructional purposes; the teacher typically has a range of decisions to make in determining how to use a simulation. Drill and practice programs and tutorial programs do not usually provide so many options for their use in the classroom. As alluded to earlier, one of the most critical decisions that has to be made in using a simulation is how to measure its effects on the learning of the students. It is important to know if the intended instructional objective of the teacher has been communicated to the students. It is at least equally important, however, to measure the unintended instructional objectives that have been communicated; that is, exactly what did the students learn about the processes being modeled? Because the students (the users) are in control of specifying many of the values of the variables, they may have pursued the model in directions that the teacher did not intend, but that the model itself can certainly support. Teachers must look for such unintentional learning, both as a way of evaluating the effectiveness of the simulation itself and as a measure of the information that students will take with them into later instructional activities.

Fourth, the time required to complete a simulation is considerably more than the time required for either drill and practice or tutorial programs. Many decisions are typically required from the user of a simulation, and the user must have sufficient time to reason out the decisions and to reflect on the consequences of those decisions. Hurrying students through a simulation may reduce the learning experience to the level of a challenging drill, and that would defeat the primary purpose of a simulation activity.

Fifth, the level of interaction among students will be much greater than in drill and practice or in tutorial programs. Students should, for the most part, be working together on a simulation so that they can check their processes and decision making during the course of the program. Acquiring information on processes typically requires lots of feedback, and in simulations peers can provide some of the support mechanisms for this feedback.

MEASURING LEARNING IN A SIMULATION

It is difficult to measure the effects of a simulation on students' learning. Measuring the effects of drill and practice programs or of tutorial programs is relatively easy; their intents are fairly narrowly focused, content communication. Getting at the processes that students acquire from using simulations, however, is much more difficult.

One way to do this is to set up situations similar to those in the simulation and ask students to specify inputs that would cause given events to occur; that is, students are asked to carry out part of the simulation and, perhaps, to predict what would happen as a result of their decisions. This technique can be adapted to paper-and-pencil format, or it could be run on a computer. For example, in a nuclear reactor simulation students might be asked to identify the variables to alter, and to specify the values of those variables, in order to cool down a reactor that has begun to overheat. The teacher might not be interested in the specific values that the student gives, but rather in the directions of the changes of values of those variables; if the student has identified the proper variables and has altered those variables in the proper directions, then the teacher may decide that the simulation has in fact communicated the appropriate relationships. This kind of "test" question could be prepared in paper-and-pencil form so that each student has the same conditions to work with.

This technique does suffer from one possible defect: it may simply be measuring the practice effect of executing the simulation. Gerlach and Reiser (1976), for example, said essentially this in a review of noncomputer simulation games; students learned to "play the game" but did not seem easily able to transfer what they learned to standard school tasks. On the other hand, designing new situations that would require or encourage students to use the same processes as are modeled in the simulation is usually a very time-consuming and/or difficult task. Authors of simulations probably should have the responsibility for creating these parallel situations; it should not fall to the teacher who wants to use the simulation.

Another way to measure the effects of a simulation is to examine the outcomes of several runs through the computer simulation itself. A teacher could set a goal for the end of the simulation—for example, building up reserves of $6.00 in an eight-day simulation of a lemonade stand—and students could be given three attempts to reach this goal. Although this seems to be a fairly objective way to evaluate the understanding of the students, it too suffers from the same "practice problem" discussed earlier. Since a goal has become the criterion for success, students may be discouraged from focusing on the processes involved in reaching that goal. There certainly will be several ways to reach the goal, and the teacher may not have any clear idea of which way(s) students choose to progress toward it.

A third way to measure the effects of a simulation is to watch the students play it; that is, observe the processes that students are using as they interact with it. Questions could be interjected to probe their understanding of what they are doing and why they are doing it. This may be the most enlightening of the ways, but it obviously takes an enormous amount of time, even for only a few students. Consequently, it is not reasonable for a regular classroom teacher with a stereotypical class of twenty to thirty students.

A compromise among these possible ways of measuring the effects of simulations is perhaps the best solution that can be offered at this time. Some observation of students is necessary, at least during the first few times that the simulation is used. By sampling student behavior, the teacher can become sensitized to the learning that is going on. Setting outcome goals and then giving students a chance to reach those goals might encourage interchange of information among students about the processes that are effective in reaching those goals. Peer teaching in these situations may indeed be a very powerful way for students to understand the simulation. After all, they are approaching the simulation from a standpoint of relative ignorance about the interactions of the variables; their task is to try to identify the ways the variables interact. The teacher, on the other hand, is likely approaching the simulation from a position of relatively good understanding of the theoretical interactions that are supposed to be modeled by the simulation. Teacher communication of the relationships may implicitly give away more substance about the theoretical interactions than the simplified version in the simulation actually supports. It is important not to expect the simulation to communicate too much about the underlying theory; the simulation is only a simplified schematic instance of that underlying theory.

In addition to observation of students while they play, use of a paper-and-pencil "test" will likely prove useful in measuring the learning effects on the class as a whole. Of particular interest is whether the students who quickly reached the teacher-specified goals actually demonstrate use of the processes that the teacher intended to be learned.

A teacher can increase the likelihood that the intended learning outcomes will be reached by providing substantial classroom support for the simulation. This support can be provided in three ways: (a) setup, (b) monitoring, and (c) debriefing. Setup is necessary to focus students' attention on the processes that are important and on the variables that are involved in the simulation. Since the simulation environment is so rich in potential, and since students will tend to approach the simulation in ignorance, they need to be given some assistance on how to separate the relevant from the irrelevant information. The rules of the interactions (for example, the limits on the values of the variables) need to be discussed so that the students can focus on the interactions themselves and not simply on the mechanics of making the simulation operate.

Monitoring the simulation, in ways that have already been discussed, is one means by which the teacher can determine if it is teaching the intended outcomes. If not, the teacher may need to intervene to refocus attention on the relevant attributes of the simulation. One risk in using simulations is that a student will discover some peculiar combination of values that causes something very unusual to happen. The "grapevine" in the classroom is frequently very effective at encouraging sharing of this kind of information. However, it may be a serious distraction to the intended instructional objectives of the simulation. The teacher must then make a decision on whether to intervene to bring the students back to the intended task or to use that unusual event as a springboard for discussion of the larger situation involved.

Debriefing is important to determine some of the things that students learned and to allow them to share their learnings. One important problem-solving heuristic is looking back at a solution to determine if there are ways of improving it or if other solutions could be used. Students can help each other make these determinations during a debriefing session.

Measuring learning resulting from a simulation activity is difficult. As noted by Gerlach and Reiser (1976), research on simulations has often omitted a clear specification of exactly what the students were supposed to learn. Without this specification, learning is likely to be missed or at least mismeasured. The problem of measuring effects of simulations is quite specific to each simulation. Teachers must be alert to this problem and plan prior to use of the simulation for measuring appropriate learning outcomes. There is much potential for learning inherent in the concept of simulations, but correspondingly serious attention must be given to finding ways to measure that potential.

SIMULATIONS IN THE PRIMARY GRADES

Given the students' level of sophistication at dealing with content in the primary grades, there will be relatively few opportunities to use simulations. Most simulations require, at a minimum, fairly good reading skills as a critical part of the interaction, and young children may not have sufficient skills to engage in this kind of interaction. Too, the cognitive level of primary-grade children may be too low to allow them to interpret relationships among variables accurately.

A few simulations, however, especially in the area of simple "economics" might be appropriate—for example, running a store or a small business. After all, "playing store" has always been a popular activity in these grades. Most uses of this activity have been to learn standard content, such as making change. Partly this emphasis is because of the difficulty in monitoring and measuring understanding of relationships among important variables, but, more critically, when primary-grade students themselves have all of the responsibilities of carrying out a simulation of a store, no one can be sure that the variables are being dealt with accurately. By having the computer run

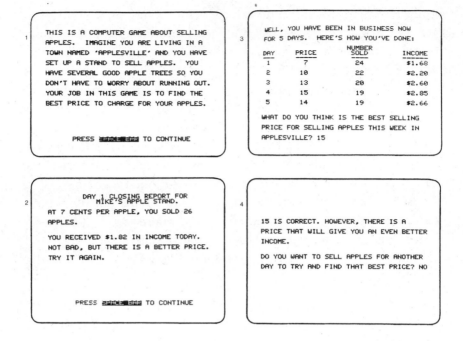

Figure 5.1 Apple stand simulation

From MECC, *Elementary*, Volume 3, pages 22–23.

the simulation, the teacher can be sure that the variables interact properly. The teacher and the students can then focus their attention on understanding the relationships.

One appropriate simulation is Sell Apples (MECC, 1980a). This simulation involves only two variables, price and sales, but only one of these, namely price, is under the control of the user. Clearly the simulation is too simple, and it thus runs the risk of teaching marginally incorrect concepts, so the teacher is encouraged in the print support materials to help students identify other variables that may play a role in running a fruit stand in the real world. These additional variables probably cannot be studied thoroughly, but the students can at least be sensitized to the potential oversimplification of the program.

The print support materials provided with this simulation are one of its strengths. Explanations are provided for the teacher on how to prepare for the simulation (setup), how to use the simulation in class (monitor progress) through both whole-class demonstration and small-group or individual decision making, and how to follow up through class discussion (debriefing) after everyone has used the simulation. These materials would have to be adapted to fit the maturity of a particular group of students, but the outline is provided to aid in effective lesson-planning.

A simulation like this one might best be used as part of a unit on roles that people play in society. Business people provide services to the community, but they are faced with a multitude of decisions in order to remain solvent. One of these decisions is how to set a price for a product, and that decision in turn affects the amount of product that they sell. Finding the best price, if total profit is the goal, is difficult and may often be a trial-and-error event. This simulation would help students gain a feel for that.

SIMULATIONS IN THE
INTERMEDIATE GRADES

There are many simulations that might be used in the intermediate grades, for example, Lemonade Stand (Apple, 1979), Oregon (MECC, 1980c), and Odell Lake (MECC, 1980b). These cover content, respectively, in economics, social studies, and science. Since many of the students will not yet be in the formal operations stage, some difficulty may be encountered with any simulation that deals with more than two or three variables. If the number of combinations of values of variables becomes too large, students may not be able to deal systematically with all of the possibilities.

One appropriate program for the intermediate grades is Sell Bicycles (MECC, 1980a), which is a more sophisticated simulation of running a store. It involves several variables: production level, advertising budget, and selling price (all under the control of the user), production cost (fixed each quarter by the program), and random events, such as a burglary (completely controlled by the program). Two "companies" compete against each other, the first to reach a fixed level of assets being the winner.

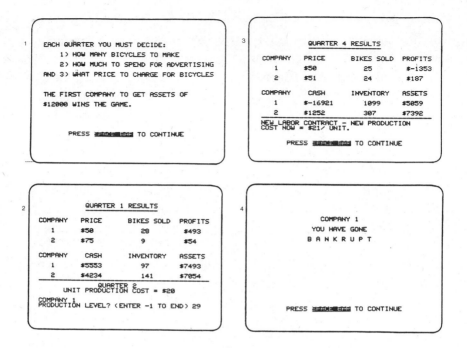

Figure 5.2 Bicycle store simulation

From MECC, *Elementary*, Volume 3, pages 37–38.

Again, Sell Bicycles offers a variety of print support materials for both the teacher and the student, not only for use during the simulation (e.g., record-keeping sheets) but also as follow-up activities (e.g., problem-solving tasks). This simulation, like all others, depends for its effectiveness on substantial teacher support. Focusing students' attention on relationships is not a simple task, but it is an important one.

A more fancily packaged simulation is Oh, Deer! (MECC, 1983), which involves management of a deer population over a five-year period. The variables involved in this simulation are not so obvious as in the previous example; the user may not clearly understand how decisions affect the changes in deer populations. Thus, debriefing for this simulation becomes very important.

After being presented with some preliminary information, the user must make a management decision for the first year (Figures 5.3 and

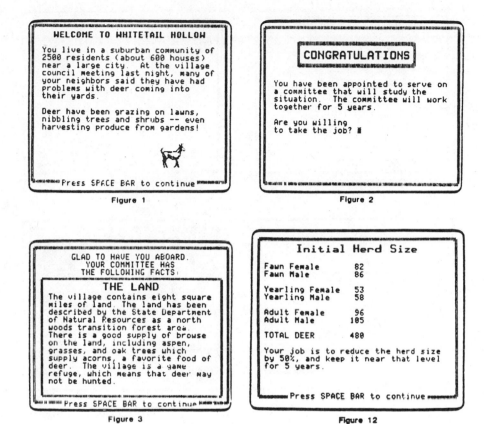

Figure 5.3 Preliminary information

From MECC, *Oh, Deer!*, pages 4, 6.

5.4). After each year, feedback is provided so that progress can be charted. The feedback even includes citizen approval rates (Figure 5.5). As in Sell Bicycles, there are random events—for example, a fire—and at the end of the five-year period a summary chart is provided (Figures 5.6 and 5.7).

The support materials for Oh, Deer! are extensive. They even include study materials for students (and teachers, too) on principles of wildlife management. Few other simulations give this kind of support, even though it is probably essential for effective use of any simulation.

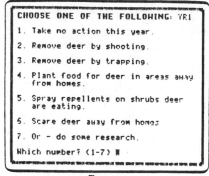

```
CHOOSE ONE OF THE FOLLOWING: YR1

1. Take no action this year.

2. Remove deer by shooting.

3. Remove deer by trapping.

4. Plant food for deer in areas away
   from homes.

5. Spray repellents on shrubs deer
   are eating.

6. Scare deer away from homes

7. Or - do some research.

Which number? (1-7) ▮
```

Figure 13

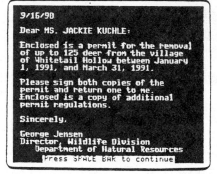

```
You have chosen to take no action
this year. Residents continue to
feed deer, causing the animals to
stay near homes.
```

Press SPACE BAR to continue

Figure 14

```
The permit request will contain the
following information.  Enter each
item and press <RETURN>.

┌────────────────────────────────────┐
│ TODAY'S DATE IS: 9/9/90            │
│                                    │
│ YOUR FULL NAME?                    │
│ JACKIE KUCHLE                      │
│                                    │
│ MR. OR MS.? MS                     │
│                                    │
│ NUMBER OF DEER THE COMMITTEE WILL  │
│ ATTEMPT TO REMOVE? 125▮            │
└────────────────────────────────────┘
```

Figure 15

```
9/16/90

Dear MS. JACKIE KUCHLE:

Enclosed is a permit for the removal
of up to 125 deer from the village
of Whitetail Hollow between January
1, 1991, and March 31, 1991.

Please sign both copies of the
permit and return one to me.
Enclosed is a copy of additional
permit regulations.

Sincerely,

George Jensen
Director, Wildlife Division
   Department of Natural Resources
Press SPACE BAR to continue
```

Figure 16

Figure 5.4　Choosing actions

From MECC, *Oh, Deer!*, page 7.

CONCLUSION

Computers in the classroom provide an opportunity to use simulations that simply wouldn't exist without the computers' capabilities. No teacher could even hope to be expert enough in all areas to develop appropriate simulations in them all. Too, noncomputer simulations typically require so much computation by users to determine the consequences of decisions that the simulation becomes too much drudgery. By having the computer take over the drudgery part and by relying on the author of the program to possess the knowledge to make the simulation more or less accurate, the teacher is freed to focus on the instructional use of the simulation.

```
┌─────────────────────────────────────┐
│ SPRING RESULTS, BEFORE FAWNING       │
│                                       │
│ Fawn Female          88               │
│ Fawn Male            96               │
│                                       │
│ Yearling Female      59               │
│ Yearling Male        68               │
│                                       │
│ Adult Female        133               │
│ Adult Male          153               │
│                                       │
│ TOTAL DEER          597               │
│                                       │
│ Your team removed 21 deer.            │
│                                       │
│ A moderate winter contributed to 140  │
│ deaths, including natural deaths,     │
│ car kills, and dog kills.             │
│                                       │
│ ══════ Press SPACE BAR to continue ══ │
└─────────────────────────────────────┘
```

Figure 21

```
┌─────────────────────────────────────┐
│ FALL POPULATION                       │
│                                       │
│ Population Class YR1 YR2 YR3 YR4 YR5  │
│                                       │
│ Fawn Female       96 125 134          │
│ Fawn Male        104 136 145          │
│                                       │
│ Yearling Female   49  80  88          │
│ Yearling Male     51  87  96          │
│                                       │
│ Adult Female     122 159 192          │
│ Adult Male       133 171 221          │
│                                       │
│ TOTAL DEER       555 758 876          │
│                                       │
│ Herd currently OVER ideal herd size   │
│                                       │
│ Have you recorded this information?   │
│ (yes or no) ▌                         │
└─────────────────────────────────────┘
```

Figure 22

```
┌─────────────────────────────────────┐
│         COST TO RESIDENTS             │
│              YEAR 3                    │
│                                       │
│                                       │
│ Management Method......  $3,840.00    │
│                                       │
│ Damages                               │
│ - Car/Deer Collisions.. $32,685.00    │
│ - Landscape Damage..... $31,680.00    │
│                                       │
│ TOTAL.................. $68,205.00    │
│                                       │
│                                       │
│                                       │
│ ══════ Press SPACE BAR to continue ══ │
└─────────────────────────────────────┘
```

Figure 23

Press SPACE BAR to continue

Figure 24

Figure 5.5   Feedback

From MECC, *Oh, Deer!*, page 9.

Because simulations are so new to the classroom, research on their effectiveness is only beginning. Generalization of results of research on noncomputer simulations, mostly at the college level, suggests that positive effects will not frequently be found. However, the most critical learning effect of simulations, namely, understanding of relationships

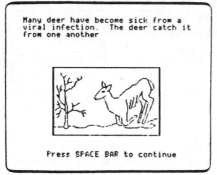

Figure 25

Figure 26

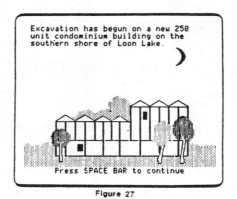

Figure 27

Figure 5.6   Random events

From MECC, *Oh, Deer!*, page 10.

among variables, have often been ignored in that research. Perhaps by focusing attention on these understandings, teachers can demonstrate both that simulations really do teach and that students can learn this cognitively sophisticated content much earlier than perhaps most people would expect.

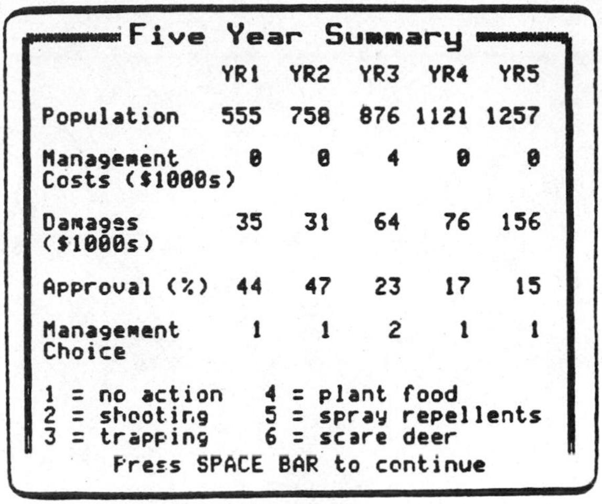

```
┌──────────────────────────────────────┐
│ ▬▬▬▬▬ Five Year Summary ▬▬▬▬▬         │
│          YR1   YR2   YR3   YR4   YR5  │
│                                       │
│ Population  555   758   876  1121 1257│
│                                       │
│ Management    0     0     4     0    0│
│ Costs ($1000s)                        │
│                                       │
│ Damages      35    31    64    76  156│
│ ($1000s)                              │
│                                       │
│ Approval (%) 44    47    23    17   15│
│                                       │
│ Management    1     1     2     1    1│
│ Choice                                │
│                                       │
│ 1 = no action    4 = plant food       │
│ 2 = shooting     5 = spray repellents │
│ 3 = trapping     6 = scare deer       │
│       Press SPACE BAR to continue     │
└──────────────────────────────────────┘
```

Figure 28

Figure 5.7   Summary information

From MECC, *Oh, Deer!*, page 11.

Diagnosis of Errors

6

Classroom instruction is typically paced for the group (class) rather than for each individual in the group. Consequently, both lost learning and incorrect learning may unintentionally be created in a class. The former might cause gaps in performance (e.g., I don't know what to do next.) while the latter may be exhibited in incorrect responses (e.g., The plural of goose is gooses.). Diagnosis is a means for identifying both lost and incorrect learning. After a correct diagnosis has been made, remediation can be focused on the precise difficulties that a student is having rather than on a general set of possible difficulties that might or might not apply to a particular student. Ideally, such remediation will be both effective at correcting the difficulty and efficient of the student's and the teacher's time.

Diagnosis procedures are certainly applicable to a wide range of elementary school content; for example, mathematics, science, language arts. However, because of the novelty of diagnosis techniques, and because more work seems to have been done in diagnosis in mathematics, most of the examples in this chapter will deal with mathematics.

WHAT IS DIAGNOSIS?

Diagnosis in this situation is any procedure that a teacher can use to determine the lost or incorrect learning. Typically, it is accomplished either through personal interviews of students while they are working or through examination of responses on specially designed tests. Either procedure requires considerable time of the teacher. In the first case, in fact, the teacher must not only spend time interviewing students but also arrange for some self-directed activity for the rest of the students in the class. In the second case, because students are not physically present to explain the work that has already been done, the teacher must make many inferences about what they might have been doing; the teacher does not have the option of presenting more exercises for students to complete as a check on those inferences.

Hopkins (1978) noted that "it would appear that a teacher could spend the entire year diagnosing particular strengths and weaknesses of children, at the expense of the introduction of new skills and concepts" (p. 49). Sovchik and Heddens (1978) also noted that "there may be some time for in-depth diagnosis but an in-depth case study for each student in a class of thirty is impractical" (p. 47). This suggests that some other means of performing diagnoses needs to be developed for teachers so that diagnosis becomes a regular part of the elementary school classroom.

It is important to recognize that there is a difference between an ERROR and a MISTAKE. A mistake is an incorrect answer given in response to a particular exercise or question. An error, on the other hand, is a consistent pattern of mistakes made in response to a series of similar exercises or questions. For example, a response of $6 \times 0 = 6$ is a mistake; but the set of responses, $0 \times 5 = 5$, $2 + 0 = 2$, $9 \times 0 = 9$, and $6 \times 0 = 6$, is an error, possibly indicating confusion of multiplication and addition basic facts when one of the terms or factors is zero. One mistake may or may not require remediation, but an error always does, since it represents a misunderstanding of a concept or skill. Diagnosis is designed to determine the errors (not the mistakes) that a student is making so that they can be corrected.

One of the reasons that errors are typically difficult to remediate is that most errors produce the correct answer to some exercises. For example, the confusion of addition and multiplication described above actually gives the correct answers for addition basic facts. The student may not consciously recognize that there is any confusion in her/his procedure, so each time a correct answer is reinforced, the entire wrong process is being strengthened in the student's mind. This more-or-less random reinforcement is very powerful in shaping behavior. Teachers may be unaware of the frequency with which they unintentionally reinforce wrong processes.

Ginsburg (in press) has identified five types of diagnosis: normative comparison (e.g., comparison of a student's addition skills with other students' skills), testing for performance (e.g., identifying whether a student can add with carry), cognitive analysis (e.g., identifying the processes used in adding), assessment of learning potential (e.g., identifying whether a student is capable of learning to add), and obtaining an integrative portrait (e.g., identifying the psychological processes that characterize a student's functioning in mathematics). The error diagnosis procedures discussed in this chapter apply only to the first three types of diagnosis. The last two are so little studied that trying to develop computer programs to accomplish them is very premature.

HOW CAN COMPUTERS DIAGNOSE?

One possible technique for performing diagnosis is to create computer programs that can perform a diagnosis. This diagnosis might be a separate program designed only to provide an indication of the errors a student is making, or it might be part of other instructional software. Some diagnostic programs have already been written on an experimental level, but incorporating diagnosis into regular CAI materials is in a very primitive stage.

Travis (1978), Woerner (1980), and Travis and Carry (1983) have all given attention to the development of diagnostic computer programs. In essence their approach is for students to complete a special paper-and-pencil diagnostic test and then to type the answers into a special computer program. That program matches the particular responses typed in with responses stored in the program, which are examples of particular pre-identified errors. When the student's responses match these predicted wrong answers, then a diagnostic message can be given either to the student or the teacher, or a particular remediation activity can be specified for the student. This procedure for computer diagnosis of errors takes the task of analyzing a diagnostic test away from the teacher and gives it to a computer. The student, however, still has to complete the diagnostic test in paper-and-pencil form before there is any interaction with the computer.

A perhaps better technique would be to let the student interact with the computer and have the computer analyze his or her work almost instantaneously, much as an interviewer would do in a one-on-one situation. This is technically more difficult to program, since the programmer does not know beforehand exactly what form the student's work might take. This technique also requires fairly great computer power, and it may not be possible to implement it on all microcomputers because of their limited capabilities.

One version of this technique for addition basic facts has been developed by Jensen (1982). His program provides some remediation, but if that remediation is unsuccessful, the program "locks up" the keyboard and prevents the student from continuing until the teacher has intervened. The program identifies for the teacher the error (or perhaps the mistake) the student is making, and the teacher can choose to remediate it off-line or to work through the program with the student. Neither the programming techniques nor the logic behind the program, however, were explained.

Another implementation of this technique has been proposed by Bright (1984a) and has been incorporated experimentally into a CAI program that provides drill and practice on multiplication of decimals (Bright, 1984b). The approach used depends on a thorough analysis and determination of almost all of the errors that might be made by students in performing this skill. These errors are incorporated into the program so that as each problem is generated, the computer can compute the particular wrong responses that students are likely to make. Each response of the student is matched to this list of potential wrong answers, and whenever a match is found, that information is stored. When enough matches are made with any particular error, the computer describes that error for the student and then explains why that error is not correct.

Another approach to diagnosis has been taken by Brown and Burton (1978). They modeled student errors in the subtraction algorithm by breaking down the steps of that algorithm into small units and then reconstructing incorrect student processes by combining these units in various ways. In the description by Barclay (1982) of a resulting program, called BUGGY, a series of incorrectly worked exercises is presented. When the user signals to the computer that s/he knows what the error is, the computer asks for a written (typed) description of the error and then checks the solution by presenting more problems for the user to work in the same incorrect way. If the user's incorrect answers match the computer's, the user is credited with a correct analysis. The program has no way to analyze the written description given by the user.

WHEN SHOULD COMPUTER DIAGNOSIS BE USED?

In some situations it is important for the teacher to take students aside and determine the particular difficulty that they are having. In these cases the proper computer use would be a program that only provides the diagnosis. This would seem most appropriate when a student has repeatedly been unable to learn material either through whole-class instruction or through whatever individualized attention the teacher has been able to give. Such behavior would indicate that there is a fundamental misunderstanding about the material that needs to be corrected. (Of course there is the possibility that the student has a learning disability, but this book will not address the ways that such learning disabilities can be identified.)

A second and potentially very effective way of using computer diagnostic capabilities is to incorporate those capabilities into ordinary CAI. For example, in a drill and practice program on alphabetizing words, it would be possible to determine systematic errors that a student is making (e.g., reverses the order of P and Q). By making this determination after only a few practice exercises, it would be possible for the program to provide remediation of those errors before they were embedded in the student's cognition.

The effort needed to remediate these errors as they are first being developed is presumably considerably less than the effort needed to remediate them after the student has practiced the wrong procedures many times. That is, the amount of "unlearning" for the student is quite a bit less if the errors can be detected as they are developing. This would help combat one of the frequent criticisms of typical individualized programs; namely, that the student is left to her/his own devices too much of the time. Students can develop wrong procedures that work often enough so that the students may not be aware that the procedures are not wholly correct. By the time the teacher finds out, the effort needed to remediate the errors is enormous.

Diagnostic capability could be built into any kind of CAI—drill and practice, tutorial, simulation, or game. Whenever students are asked to do the same kind of exercise repeatedly, there is the possibility that they will do the exercise with some kind of incorrect process. That is the situation in which diagnostic capability is desirable.

Too, so little is known about how students remember information that even if they have demonstrated mastery previously, there is the possibility that new errors will creep into their work. These new errors may go undetected for a long time simply because the teacher expects that the work will be correct and may attribute any mistakes to "carelessness."

In a drill and practice program, in particular, it seems essential that diagnostic procedures be built in, if the quality of such programs is to increase significantly. Drill and practice is designed to be used either to firm up a student's skill or understanding of a topic early in the learning of that topic, or it is designed to help a student maintain skill or understanding. In the first case the student's performance is likely to vary quite a bit. If the errors that are exhibited are not caught early, the student may actually learn the wrong skill. In the second case interference in remembering the correct processes may occur because of new material that has been learned since the particular skill was first mastered. Diagnosis at this point in teaching would be designed to eliminate such interference.

Tutorials, because they are designed to teach new material, usually check to be sure that the concepts or skills are not learned incorrectly. Hence, most tutorial programs give considerable attention to finding out what students are actually learning and to correcting whatever misunderstanding may have developed. This is typically done by careful selection of questions that give students opportunities to make the most common mistakes. Remediation is provided whenever a response is given that matches one of these common errors. In some sense this is not quite diagnosis, since there is usually not a sequence of similar mistakes to diagnose. Tutorials might be made more effective, however, if more opportunities were provided for students to demonstrate mistakes in a sequence of exercises. The development of techniques for incorporating diagnosis into CAI will give authors of tutorials the chance to make more accurate diagnoses based on a series of exercises rather than on only a few carefully chosen questions.

Games and simulations typically assume that students understand the content necessary to participate. In most cases this assumption is justified, and in most circumstances any diagnostic procedure that is built into such a program would not be needed. If a student responds correctly to all of the exercises, there is nothing to diagnose. However, for those students who have not learned the content, diagnosis might be especially helpful.

WHAT GOES INTO A DIAGNOSIS PROGRAM?

The primary difference between a computer diagnosis program and a teacher-administered procedure is that the computer program must be totally self-contained. A teacher who encounters an unexpected student response can evaluate that response and make an at least reasonably appropriate reply based on previous experience with the content and with students. Computers, on the other hand, can only process responses within the limits of what has been built into the program itself. Hence, procedures must be programmed so that all student responses get replies that make sense.

The first step in designing a diagnosis program is to make a clear delimitation of the content to be diagnosed. If too much content is included, the program will fast become too complicated, for there will be too many potential errors to deal with.

Second, curriculum practices for the content must be identified. These include sequencing of prerequisite material, sequencing of instructional moves, and identifying the symbolism used to communicate the material. Some errors may be directly related to a particular sequence of presenting the material, and this must be taken into account in the program.

Third, potential errors that students might make must be listed. One source of this information is the literature on student errors, but other sources are analysis of the content itself and previous experience in teaching the content to students. This last source is particularly important if the errors are related to particular instructional strategies. This step in developing a diagnosis program is probably the most critical for having a program that is usable. Initial trials of any diagnosis program will reveal errors that were overlooked; such initial trials are essential before a diagnosis program is made commercially available.

Fourth, a procedure must be developed for turning a student's wrong responses into a specification of the error(s) being committed. This procedure must be completely algorithmic, for it must become part of the computer program. This is probably the most difficult part of writing a computer diagnosis program, but without such a procedure, there could be no diagnosis program. As more research is conducted on the development of diagnosis programs, a variety of techniques will become available for programmers to use, and as programmers gain experience with diagnosis programs, the procedures will become more efficient and more sophisticated. These procedures have to do what an experienced teacher might do in analyzing the mistakes to identify the underlying error.

Fifth, the program must keep records of the student's performance and the particular diagnosis determined. Such records would be useful to the classroom teacher for follow-up with students who are having severe difficulties. With even current microcomputer technology, such records can be kept unobtrusively on disk so that the teacher can retrieve them after the student has completed the program.

Sixth, a diagnosis program should provide some documentation for the teacher on how remediation might be accomplished. This might be in the form of a user's manual or it might be automatically stored along with the records of a student's performance, so that as a teacher retrieves those records the remediation suggestions are automatically printed out.

Finally, as the curriculum changes and as research reveals new information, understanding of the possible causes of mistakes may also change. That is, the particular mistakes may not change, but the underlying errors may be reconceptualized. For example, mistakes that in the early twentieth century were viewed primarily as careless have more recently been viewed as instances of incorrect but consistently applied, student-developed algorithms. Currently, evidence is mounting that those errors may reflect algorithms that are incomplete, perhaps in only one place, rather than wholly incorrect (e.g., Brown and Burton, 1978). No diagnosis can be cast in stone, so provision needs to be made in any diagnosis program for upgrading the diagnosis-creating process.

EXAMPLES OF DIAGNOSIS PROGRAMS

There are very few commercial examples of diagnosis programs or of diagnosis procedures in other kinds of CAI. Thus, only two examples will be provided.

Figure 6.1 presents screen displays for a diagnostic test written in microcomputer format. The screens show a typical question that might be asked and the summary information provided at the end of the testing session. Questions for most diagnostic tests are in this multiple-choice format because of the ways that errors are diagnosed. As a result, only a few patterns in the responses of the students can typically be recognized. This severely limits the range of applicability of such a test, and if the number of patterns is too small, the student's errors may be forced to fit one of these patterns. In this case there is the risk that the diagnosis will be incorrect.

Diagnostic tests of this kind are typically built from a list of objectives that are expected to be mastered. The objectives may be in a hierarchy, with many interdependencies, but that is not necessary. They may merely be a list of things that students are supposed to be able to do. The diagnosis will indicate those objectives that have not been mastered. In the case of many dependencies, the test may abort if a student misses one or two objectives early in the hierarchy.

```
                    REPRESENTATIVE OUTPUT

Objectives Missed

            Decreasing Patterns

            Sums from 20 to 100, No Regrouping

            2-Digit and 2-Digit Subtraction, No
            Regrouping

            Factors Between Five and Ten

            One-Digit Divided by One-Digit


                    Representative Output
```

Objectives Mastered		Specific Problem Area
Number Concepts	Incrementing Sequences	Decreasing Patterns
	Estimating Division by 20	
Addition	Sums to 10	Sums from 20 to 100, No Regrouping
	Sums from 10 to 20	
Subtraction	Single Digits	2-Digit and 2-Digit, No Regrouping
	2-Digit--1 Digit	No Regrouping
Multiplication	Factors Less Than to Equal to Five	Factors Between Five and Ten
Division		One-Digit Divided by One-Digit

Interpretation

Figure 6.1 Screens from *Math Doctor*

From Barbara Signer, "A Model of Microcomputer Adaptive Diagnosis," published in the *1984 RCDPM Research Monograph*. Reprinted with permission.

Figure 6.2 presents screen displays from a drill and practice program that also diagnoses students' errors. This particular program provides a diagnosis after the same error is encountered three times. That cutoff is an instructional decision of the programmer and is not related to the design of the program.

It should again be noted that an error may also produce correct answers occasionally. The particular error diagnosed in Figure 6.2 produces the correct answer when the product of the non-zero digits has two digits, as in the case of the second exercise. Diagnosis-creating procedures must take this phenomenon into account.

HOW CAN DIAGNOSIS PROGRAMS BE USED?

The major focus in teacher education programs, both preservice and in-service, seems to be on the initial teaching act. That is, how does a teacher present information the first time? Very little attention seems to be given to identifying ways in which that same content can be retaught to students that did not learn the material through whole-class instruction. Diagnosis programs would seem to fit best into teaching sequences that emphasize the reteaching act.

To use diagnosis programs requires understanding a three-step cycle for this reteaching act. First, appropriate times in a teaching sequence need to be identified when a diagnosis program might be used. Certainly it should not be used after every mistake is encountered. Rather, major concepts and skills need to be identified which, if they are not learned correctly, will hinder the progress of students. Diagnosis programs would probably best be used at the point of teaching these major ideas.

Second, remediation techniques that attempt to correct the errors identified by the diagnosis program need to be developed as part of the teacher's repertoire. For some content (e.g., arithmetic) a wide variety of techniques are available (e.g., Ashlock, 1972). For most content, however, the techniques for remediation are scattered throughout the professional literature and presentations at professional meetings. Teachers have to work hard at finding them.

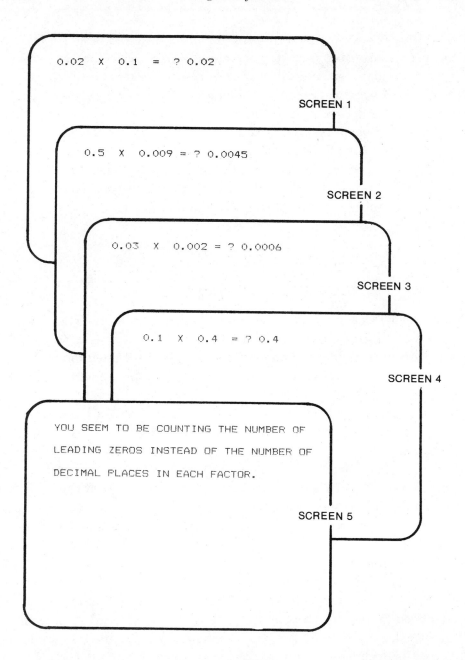

Figure 6.2   Screens from drill and practice with diagnosis

Third, teachers need to follow up on the diagnosis-remediation cycle. The effectiveness of the remediation strategies needs to be assessed, perhaps with further diagnosis.

After teachers are comfortable with this three-step cycle, they can begin to use diagnosis programs in more creative ways. One potentially very important way is as a measure of the effectiveness of their own teaching. By using a diagnosis program prior to teaching some content, the teacher can determine what understandings the students are bringing to the teaching. By using the same diagnosis program after teaching the content, the teacher can determine what understandings the students actually developed as a result of the instruction. The teacher can then identify whether the intended learning and the actual learning were the same. If not, then the instruction would need to be examined to find out possible reasons why students learned something different than what was intended.

EXAMPLES OF ERRORS IN
THE PRIMARY GRADES

Ginsburg and Allardice (1984) have reported an error made by a third-grade student; this error shows the range of behaviors that a diagnosis program must be prepared to deal with.

When asked what he is doing in school, Butch says he is working with fractions:

Interviewer: Fractions? Can you show me what you are doing with fractions?

(Butch writes 8/16.)

Interviewer: Okay. So what does that say?

Butch: 8, 16.

Interviewer: 8, 16. Okay. What do you do with it?

Butch: You add it up and put the number up there.

Interviewer: Okay. What is the number?

23

(Butch writes 8/16.)

Obviously, Butch is doing something unusual. He confuses division
with fractions, and he cannot calculate simple division. (p. 195)

More common errors are those reported by Brown and Burton (1978)
for addition; for example, misalignment and diagonal addition.

$$
\begin{array}{lr}
\text{Misalignment:} & 34 \\
& +\ \underline{3} \\
& 64 \\
\\
\text{Diagonal} & 46 \\
\text{addition:} & +\ \underline{\ 2} \\
& 68 \\
\end{array}
$$

All of these errors are potentially identifiable by computer diagnosis procedures. In the primary grades it is very important that
teachers build strong basic understandings so that learning in later
grades does not suffer. Diagnosis programs can help teachers check
on the level of understanding that students develop.

EXAMPLES OF ERRORS IN INTERMEDIATE GRADES

Behr, Lesh, Post, and Silver (1982) have extensively studied the difficulties that students have in representing fractions on a number line.
Since the number line is a pervasive model for fractions in elementary
school, it is indeed important to know the errors that students make
in dealing with that model. The errors are typically conceptual errors,
which are more difficult to identify and to remediate than errors in
algorithms. For example, identifying the wrong unit is a common
error. In Figure 6.3 a student who exhibited this error would name
X with the fraction, 4/6, rather than 4/3 or 1 1/3.

Travis (1984) has given attention to errors in the multiplication
algorithm; and although the subjects in her study were not elementary
school students, the errors are typical of those made by intermediate

Student response: X = $\dfrac{4}{6}$

Correct response: X = $\dfrac{4}{3}$

Figure 6.3   Example of mislabeling of fraction on number line

grade students. One of the most common errors seems to be the misplacement of a partial product; that is, misalignment of digits of the partial products. A misplaced partial product will have a value that is an order of magnitude off (either ten times as much as, or one-tenth the value of, the correct value). This kind of error-trapping is easily caught by a computer, whose best feature is perhaps manipulation of numerical values.

CONCLUSION

Diagnosis of errors is a use of computers that has rarely been taken advantage of by designers of educational software. It seems to have great potential for enhancing learning, but the research and development effort needed to achieve that potential is quite large. One of

```
                              409
                          x  285
                          --------
                             2045
(off by orders               3272
     of magnitude)            818
                          --------
                            6135
```

Correct product = 116565

Figure 6.4 Sample error in multiplication algorithm

the ways to push this development is by teachers' insisting that diagnosis procedures be included in most, if not all, educational software. The very limited research that has been conducted on the use
of diagnosis, in both computer and noncomputer forms, suggests that
students would benefit from its inclusion on a regular basis in
instruction.

The development of programming techniques to allow diagnosis
in software is one aspect of the growing computer science field called
artificial intelligence. The claims for the ultimate usefulness of artificial intelligence may be overblown, but until more systems are in
operation, no one will know for sure. It seems certain that it will
remain a heavily researched field for many years to come, and students
can only benefit from breakthroughs that are sure to come. Computer
diagnosis will become more and more common in educational software, but the exact implementations may not be any of those described
earlier. Teachers must simply watch for developments to occur and
be ready to take advantage of them as they happen.

Evaluating 7
Instructional Software

In principle, the goals of and the processes for evaluating instructional software (both computer-assisted instruction and utility software such as a word processor) are the same as for any kind of instructional material. However, in practice there are important differences that overshadow the similarities.

For instructional materials in print format it is easy to get an overview of the kind of instruction that is going to be provided. The entire product can be studied all at once, and a teacher can digest the essence of the instruction by skimming through the material. Although some subtleties may be overlooked this way, typically few surprises are in store for the teacher who uses the item in class. Even with films or tapes, the teacher can preview the item and be confident that the students are going to be exposed to exactly the same images that the teacher saw. One complication raised in the evaluation of films and tapes, however, is that the teacher usually cannot speed up the rate of presentation during the preview. It is not easy to skim through a film. Evaluation of these items, then, is slower than for print materials.

In addition, the evaluation of instructional software is considerably more complicated. Much of the potential instruction for a particular student is hidden inside the program, and the teacher is typically given no clue as to the kinds of alternatives that might be called into play by unique combinations of students' responses to the questions or exercises that are presented. Hence, the process of evaluating in-structional software is in a very real sense a contest, in which the teacher tries to find out how the program might adapt to various student responses.

WHAT IS THE PURPOSE OF EVALUATION?

The primary goal of evaluating instructional software is to determine if it can be used effectively in a particular classroom. As with any instructional material, the teacher must first determine if the objec-tives of the software are consistent with and complementary to the objectives already set for that classroom. Unfortunately, the objectives identified by the author of the software may not accurately reflect what the program actually teaches. Usually there are unintentional objectives of a program that only become known after some experience in using it.

For example, in most versions of Hangman one hidden objective is to make the fancy graphics appear on the screen, with the graphics appearing only when a word is misspelled. At least that is what some students seem to assume is the objective. Of course, this outcome is not only different from the stated objective of the program but also counterproductive for that stated objective. A hidden objective of this type might not become obvious to a teacher without watching children use the software over a period of time. It does suggest, however, that teachers need to be alert for subtleties of this kind even during the initial evaluation of software.

An important related concern is that the content presented in the program must be accurate. This means, for example, both that the technical content must be correct and that the manner of presenting that content (e.g., spelling, grammar) must also be correct. This is similar to looking for "typos" in printed material, but again there is the disadvantage of not being able to see the entire product at once.

Similarly, the pedagogy used to present the material should be carefully examined. For example, if a teacher were at the point of using drill and practice for completing the mastery of multiplication basic facts, then a program that went back to careful and time-consuming development of understanding of those facts would be inappropriate. Such a program would be counterproductive for the instructional goals that had been established by the teacher.

As a rule of thumb, all the considerations of instructional design that apply to other kinds of instructional materials also apply to instructional software. Roblyer (1981), for example, has been particularly effective in presenting this case to people with computer background but without much educational background. The most important aspects of this case seem to be that the instructional software should be designed in the context of what is known about how people learn and that the software should be fully tested to be sure that it teaches effectively and efficiently. The likelihood of obtaining high-quality software this way is considerably greater than through the perhaps-more-common procedure of having a computer programmer go off to write instructional software.

WHAT TO LOOK FOR IN INSTRUCTIONAL SOFTWARE

The things to look for in evaluating instructional software fall basically into three categories: instructional design, appropriate use of computer capabilities, and technical quality. Each of these categories can be further broken down in a variety of ways.

Instructional design, as already pointed out, involves the correctness of the content presented, the correctness of the manner of presentation, and the soundness of the pedagogy employed. Most teachers soon develop a "sixth sense" for instructional design flaws in printed materials. Unlike printed materials, however, instructional software must be examined for its hidden objectives. These may be prompted by the particular ways in which the computer is used or by the particular approach used to present material. In simulations, for example, the hidden objectives may be understanding some inadvertently presented relationships between the variables in the program. Identifying these hidden objectives may be difficult, and their effects may not surface with a first or even second trial run.

Appropriate use of computer capabilities is an important category to consider, especially if computing equipment is in short supply. The use of computers to provide instruction in ways that other materials could do better is wasteful of resources. Perhaps more important, however, is that an inappropriate use of computers prohibits others from using the equipment to accomplish goals that might not be attained without computers. This is wasteful of human resources and leaves teachers open to potential criticism.

There are two primary misuses of computer capabilities in the existing commercial instructional software. First, computers are too often used as electronic page-turners, and second, too many fancy graphics and sound options are used in ways that are totally extraneous to the content being presented.

Using the computer as an electronic page-turner is often the first approach beginning programmers take for developing instructional software. Two reasons for this may be: first, PRINT commands are often the first commands learned in a programming language, and they are both relatively easy to use and relatively powerful in getting information on the screen. Second, people who are just learning to program are often fascinated with the speed with which large amounts of information can be presented on a monitor screen. However, using computers to present information in this way is not very cost-effective. Printing, photocopying, and dittoing are far cheaper. The printed mode allows readers to read as quickly or as slowly as they like and to do the reading in virtually any setting; there is no need, for example, for access to an electrical outlet. A rule of thumb is that if more than three or four screensful of information are presented sequentially, the computer is not being used appropriately.

The use of too many fancy graphics and too much sound is often the second phase that programmers go through in designing instructional software. Apparently one of the strongest motivators in keeping students involved in CAI materials is the combination of graphics and sound. Hence, most beginning programmers, if they intend to produce instructional software, want to learn how to control the graphics and the sound. Once they learn how to do some creative things, they feel obliged to do so in every program they write. This obligation arises from programming concerns, however, not educational concerns.

Teachers must insist that any graphics and sound be used primarily to improve the quality of the learning and not to make the programmer feel satisfied.

Graphics and sound are most often used to provide reinforcement of correct or incorrect responses. As an occasional reinforcer, this is good educational practice, but for repeated use, such as in a drill and practice program, it is probably inappropriate. The sound and graphics start to get in the way of learning the content.

An appropriate use of graphics and sound can be seen in the program, Lemonade Stand (Apple Computer, 1979), which is a simplistic simulation of operation of a lemonade stand. At the start of each "day" a weather report is given through the dual device of a picture of the appropriate weather and the playing of a few bars of an appropriate song. One of the variables that students are supposed to keep in mind in the operation of the lemonade stand is the kind of weather for the day. Hot, dry days should result in greater demand for lemonade than cool, rainy days. However, the program designer didn't want simply to tell students that this is important. There was a need, therefore, to call attention to this variable without explicitly telling how it would be related to the goal of the simulation. The graphics together with the sound highlight the relevant information and at the same time give the students multiple means (sight and hearing) for remembering the information.

Other appropriate uses of computer technology would include use of interaction between the user and the program, diagnosis of errors in students' responses, use of flashing mode or different speeds of printing to call attention to pieces of information, drawing of diagrams to illustrate concepts, using time limits for responses in speed drills, random selection of particular exercises or questions, and immediate feedback for each response. These options cannot easily be accomplished in noncomputer environments, and there is mounting evidence that they assist the process of learning.

The technical quality of a program is somewhat more difficult to discuss without viewing instructional software. Basically, examination of technical quality is centered around the goal of keeping the software from "bombing out" while it is being run. That is, instructional software should always be protected from both intentional and unintentional misuses by students. Some students set as a goal making the program quit running before the instruction is complete. These students learn a variety of techniques for attempting to reach this goal; for example, typing in a string of letters when numbers seem to be called for, typing a number with forty or fifty digits when the expected response is much smaller, or hitting the special keys on the computer keyboard (e.g., the ESCape key or the RESET key). High-quality instructional software will take these possibilities into account within the program and will protect the program from such abuses. During the process of evaluation of software, teachers should take on the role of such students in order to determine how careful the program designer has been.

One particularly good source of information in testing the technical quality of software is the Minnesota Educational Computing Consortium (MECC). On the basis of their experience, they have produced a list of technical checks that teachers should use in evaluation of instructional software. Some of the most important of these include the following:

1. When a response is called for, press the RETURN key only. The question should be repeated or help should be given.
2. Answer a question with an extremely long string of characters. It should be processed satisfactorily.
3. Answer a question and then press the RETURN key twice, quickly. The next question or frame should not flip past.
4. Test to see that the program will accept answers that are equivalent in context (e.g., Saint Paul, St. Paul, City of St. Paul as the capital of Minnesota).
5. When information is repeated, the screen display should not "scroll"; that is, the printing should not disappear off the top of the monitor screen (MECC, 1980, p. 22).

EVALUATION FORMS

Fortunately, teachers do have some help in conducting evaluations of instructional software. A variety of evaluation forms provide a framework within which to make systematic evaluations.

```
Your Name(s):
Program Name:
```

1. How appropriate is computer use for this activity?

2. Are the goals of the program clear?   (What are they?)

3. Does the activity in the program focus on these goals?

4. Are the instructions clear?   (If not, why?)

5. How understandable is the format of the output?

6. How good is the continuity of the output?

7. How vulnerable is the program to input mistakes?

8. How appropriately is reinforcement used?

9. Are the special features of this microcomputer used well?

Figure 7.1   MECC Software Evaluation Form

MECC (1980) has developed an evaluation form that focuses on getting an overview of the software. Questions 2, 3, 4, and 8 are related to the instructional design, questions 1 and 9 are related to the appropriateness of use of the computer's capabilities, and questions 5, 6, and 7 are related to the technical quality of the software. A teacher could provide as much or as little information as necessary for future usefulness in response to these questions.

Other evaluation forms have been developed by the National Council of Teachers of Mathematics, by the publication *School Microware*

Review, and by *Electronic Learning*. These forms differ from the MECC form in that they provide a checklist of relevant questions rather than more general questions that require considerable interpretation on the part of the user. For this reason they are probably more useful for the occasional evaluation of software, such as will be done by most elementary school teachers.

All of these forms attend to the three categories important for software evaluations. The specific questions, however, are slightly different and represent slightly different emphases on various aspects of these categories. The particular evaluation form that a teacher uses as a model should be the one that will provide the most useful information when the form is read in the future, either by the same person or by other people who might want to have an opinion on a particular piece of instructional software. Probably most teachers will want to create a combination form that uses relevant questions from several available forms.

TIME NEEDED TO EVALUATE

As has already been mentioned, the time needed to evaluate adequately a piece of instructional software is considerably greater than that needed for more traditional kinds of instructional materials. The teacher needs to try out as many of the potential paths through the software as time will permit. Especially in tutorial or simulation software, the number of paths may be very large indeed, and certainly not all possible paths can be examined. However, at least some of the more representative paths do need to be traversed.

Too, the teacher occasionally needs to act like a disruptive student. It is not uncommon for software to be carefully protected against such disruptions early in the program and then for a program designer to lapse into carelessness and let a "bug" slip in later in the instruction. This may represent the theory that students will quit trying to make the program "bomb" if they are unsuccessful in doing so early in the program. As attractive as this theory seems, it probably is not accurate.

While it might be desirable for all teachers to evaluate all software that might be used in their classrooms, it is probably not possible to expect them to spend the necessary time to do this. A more feasible

NCTM SOFTWARE EVALUATION CHECKLIST

PROGRAM NAME: _____ SOURCE: _____ COST: _____

SUBJECT AREA: _____ REVIEWER'S NAME: _____ DATE: _____

1. INSTRUCTIONAL RANGE
_____ grade level(s)
_____ ability level(s)

2. INSTRUCTIONAL GROUPING FOR PROGRAM USE
_____ individual
_____ small group (size: _____)
_____ large group (size: _____)

3. EXECUTION TIME
_____ minutes (estimated) for average use

4. PROGRAM USE(S)
_____ demonstration
_____ drill or practice
_____ instructional gaming
_____ instructional management
_____ instructional support
_____ problem solving
_____ programming utility
_____ simulation
_____ testing operations
_____ tutorial
_____ whistles and bells
_____ word processing
_____ other (_____)

5. USER ORIENTATION: INSTRUCTOR'S POINT OF VIEW

	low		high	
flexibility	*	*	*	*
freedom from need to intervene or assist	*	*	*	*

6. USER ORIENTATION: STUDENT'S POINT OF VIEW

	low		high	
quality of directions (clarity)	*	*	*	*
quality of output (content and tone)	*	*	*	*
quality of screen formatting	*	*	*	*
freedom from need for external information	*	*	*	*
freedom from disruption by system errors	*	*	*	*
simplicity of user input	*	*	*	*

7. CONTENT

	low		high	
instructional focus	*	*	*	*
instructional significance	*	*	*	*
soundness or validity	*	*	*	*
compatibility with other materials used	*	*	*	*

8. MOTIVATION AND INSTRUCTIONAL STYLE

	passive		active	
type of student involvement	*	*	*	*

	low		high	
degree of student control	*	*	*	*

	none	poor		good	
use of game format	*	*	*	*	*
use of still graphics	*	*	*	*	*
use of animation	*	*	*	*	*
use of color	*	*	*	*	*
use of voice input and output	*	*	*	*	*
use of nonvoice audio	*	*	*	*	*
use of light pen	*	*	*	*	*
use of ancillary materials	*	*	*	*	*
use of _____	*	*	*	*	*

9. SOCIAL CHARACTERISTICS

	present and negative	not present	present	present and positive
competition	_____	_____	_____	_____
cooperation	_____	_____	_____	_____
humanizing of computer	_____	_____	_____	_____
moral issues or value judgments	_____	_____	_____	_____
summary of student performance	_____	_____	_____	_____

Figure 7.2 NCTM Review Form

Key to Terms: NCTM Software Evaluation Checklist

1. The grade levels and ability levels for a particular program are primarily determined by the concepts involved. Other important factors are reading level, prerequisite skills, degree of student control, and intended instructional use. It is possible for a program to be flexible enough to be used across a wide range of grade levels and ability levels.

2. Some programs are designed for use by individuals. Others have been or can be modified for participation by two or three persons at a time. Simulations or demonstrations often pose opportunities for large-group interaction. A given program may be used in more than one grouping, depending on the instructor.

3. The time required for the use of a program will vary considerably. Include loading time for cassettes. A time range is the appropriate response here.

4. Instructional programs can be categorized according to their uses. Some programs may have more than one use, thus falling into more than one of the following categories:

Demonstration: Used by a teacher for leading group discussion.

Drill or practice: Assumes that the concept or skill has been taught; merely reinforces.

Informational: Generates data but does not direct the use of those data.

Instructional gaming: Focuses on decision making within a game format; involves random events and the pursuit of a winning strategy.

Instructional management: Helps manage the learning environment by assuming major responsibility with respect to student assessment, record keeping, and generating learning prescriptions.

Instructional support: Generates instructional materials, helps locate instructional resources, or aids in selecting instructional products.

Problem solving: An algorithm that serves the problem solver during the exploration of a complex problem.

Programming utility: Programs that help write other instructional programs.

Simulation: An electronic slice of life.

Testing operations: Provides services such as item banking, test generation, test scoring, and item analysis.

Tutorial: A dialogue between student and computer on a topic that is not yet understood by the student.

Whistles and bells: Demonstrates features of the computer system—features that may be of value in instructional applications.

Word processing: Permits the efficient improvement of written materials.

5. These are factors relevant to the actual use of the program from the point of view of an instructor.

Flexibility: A program may allow the user or the instructor to adjust the program to different ability levels, degrees of difficulty, or concepts.

Intervention or assistance: A rating of "low" means considerable teacher intervention or assistance is required.

6. These are factors relevant to the actual use of the program from the point of view of a student.

Directions: The directions should be complete, readable, under the user's control (e.g., should not scroll off the screen until understood), and use appropriate examples.

Output: Program responses should be readable, understandable, and complete. If in response to student input, the output should be of an acceptable tone and consistent with the input request.

Screen formatting: The formats during a program run should not be distracting or cluttered. Labels and symbols should be meaningful within the given context.

External information: A program may require the user to have access to information other than that provided within it. This may include prerequisite content knowledge or knowledge of conventions used by the program designer as well as maps, books, models, and so on.

System errors: System errors result in the involuntary termination of the program.

Input: The user should know when, where, and in what form input is expected. Student input rather than automatic timing should prompt the presentation of new material on the screen, and specific screen areas should be reserved for such input. Characters with special meanings should be avoided; however, when they are needed, such symbols should be accompanied by explicit instruction and by a readily available "help" display regarding their use. The complexity of typed input should be minimized but should be sufficient to serve the learning objectives of the program.

7. These are matters relevant to the subject-matter content of the program.

Focus: The program topic should be clearly defined and of a scope that permits thorough treatment.

Significance: The instructional objectives of the program must be viewed as important by the instructor. Also, the program should represent a valid use of the computer's capabilities while improving the instructional process.

Soundness or validity: The concepts and terms employed should be correct, clear, and precise. Other important factors are the rate of presentation, degree of difficulty, and internal consistency.

Compatibility: The content, terminology, teaching style, and educational philosophy of the program should not conflict with those generally encountered by the student.

8. These items are self-explanatory.

9. Competition, cooperation, and values are concerns that may be a function of the way a program expresses them. (War gaming and the "hangman" format are sample issues.) Also, the "humanizing" of the computer may serve for motivation or to reduce anxiety, but it also may become tedious, misleading, and counterproductive.

The summary of student performance can be dichotomous (win or lose), statistical (time expended or percent of items correct), or subjective (as in the evaluation of a simulation). It may be for student, teacher, or both.

Figure 7.2 *(continued)*

SCHOOL MICROWARE EVALUATION FORM   (COPY AS NEEDED)

Your Name_____Organization_____Position_____

Address_____Tel:_____

Product Name_____Supplier_____Price $_____No. of Progs.
                                                                            Under This Name_____
School Departments
to Which Applicable_____

INSTRUCTIONS - For open ended items, supply all information requested in blanks provided if possible; use extra sheets if necessary. For objective items (those with blanks to left), enter a number in the blank to indicate the extent to which the program fulfills the description in the item, as follows: 2 - Completely, 1 - Partially, 0 - Not at All. If the item is not applicable to the program, enter N/A. If the item is unclear, enter U. Elaborate on answers as necessary in Comments section at end or on extra sheets, giving item numbers.

FUNCTIONAL DESCRIPTION - Describe the program briefly in terms of its goals and what it does to achieve them (no evaluation here).
_____
_____
_____

PRELIMINARY CONSIDERATION - Assuming that this program contributes to the teaching of one or more topics, is that topic one which is or should be taught in today's schools?___Yes___No If not, give your reasons for this answer in the Comments section at the end of the form and omit the balance of the questionnaire.

DOCUMENTATION - List materials accompanying the program, e.g., teachers guide, student workbook.
   1. Indicate types of information included.
_____   a. Suggested course/subject, grade levels.
_____   b. Goals.
_____   c. Performance objectives.
_____   d. Suggested teaching strateg(ies).
_____   e. Correlation with standard texts.
_____   f. Prerequisites for use of program.
_____   g. Student exercises, teacher answers.
_____   h. Operating instructions.
_____   i. Listing and sample runs of program(s).
_____   j. If a simulation, description of the model used.
_____   k. Suggested topics for follow-up discussions.
_____   l. Suggested references/activities for follow-up.
_____   2. The documentation is written clearly.
_____   3. If a workbook is included, the format and content are appropriate.

INSTRUCTIONS GIVEN TO USER BY PROGRAM
   1. The instructions are adequate regarding:
_____   a. The instructional task to be performed.
_____   b. Details of how to interact with the program.
_____   2. User has the option of skipping instructions if already known.

STUDENT-COMPUTER DIALOG
   1. Output is displayed screen by screen
_____   (paged) rather than scrolled.
   2. If output is paged:
_____   a. User has control over continuing to the next page.
_____   b. Amount of information in each page is appropriate.
_____   c. The perceptual impact (amount of type and lines) is suitable.
_____   3. Output is spaced and formatted so as to be easily readable.

   4. Language is well suited to most students'
_____   reading ability.
   5. Uses correct grammar,spelling,
_____   hyphenation and punctuation.
   6. Any grid or coordinate system used is
_____   consistent with common conventions.
   7. Students can respond with common symbols &
_____   ways of using them, e.g., right to left entry of sums.
   8. Accepts abbreviations for common
_____   responses.
   9. Provides for individual needs, e.g.,
_____   opportunity to work with harder or easier material.
  10. Dialog is personalized, i.e., makes
_____   appropriate use of student names.
  11. Uses devices to get & maintain interest,
_____   e.g., variation of computer responses, humor, pace change, surprise.
  12. Makes good use of any special features of computer:
       a. Graphics   b. Color   c. Sound
      _____   _____   _____
  13. Reinforcing responses (indications of
_____   right, wrong, etc.) are appropriate.
  14. The number of wrong answers allowed is
_____   reasonable.
  15. Responds appropriately if allowed number
_____   of wrong answers is exceeded.
  16. Provides opportunity to get help if
_____   difficulty is encountered.
  17. Minimizes bad entries via devices such as
_____   objective formats (multiple choice,etc).
  18. Deals well with inappropriate entries,
_____   i.e., response to typing errors, etc., is intelligible and useful.
  19. Required entries are within students'
_____   capabilities (esp. typing, vocabulary).
  20. Reports student performance periodically
_____   and at end of session.

MISCELLANEOUS CONCERNS
   1. If a simulation, the program gives a
_____   sufficiently accurate representation of the situation simulated.
   2. The concepts and vocabulary required to
_____   use the program are reasonable.
_____   3. Operates properly and is free of bugs.

   4. Is well structured and documented
_____   internally to facilitate any necessary debugging/modification.

COMMENTS - Please use this space and additional sheets as necessary to provide any other information which you believe would help someone who was considering acquiring the program being reviewed. In particular, indicate what you like least and most about the program. Also, list any changes which should be made.)
_____
_____
_____

Revised 7/81   61

Figure 7.3   School Microware Review Form

Software Evaluation Form

Reviewer's Name: _____ Date of Review: _____

Address/Phone: _____ (___) _____

Program Title _____ Medium: ___5" disk; ___8" disk;

_____ ___cartridge; ___tape

Package Title _____ Copyright Date (if any) _____

Microcomputer (brand, model, memory) _____

Necessary Hardware _____ Necessary Software _____

Producer _____ Author(s) _____

Back-up Copy Policy _____ Cost _____

PART 1

Program Overview and Description

1. Subject area and specific topic _____
2. Prerequisite skills necessary _____
3. Appropriate grade level (circle) 1 2 3 4 5 6 7 8 9 10 11 12 college
4. Type of program (check one or more)
   ___Simulation   ___Testing
   ___Educational Game   ___Classroom Management
   ___Drill and Practice   ___Other (specify) _____
   ___Tutorial   _____
   ___Problem Solving   ___Remediation
   ___Authoring System   ___Enrichment
5. Appropriate group instructional size: ___individual ___small group ___class
6. Is this program an appropriate instructional use of the computer? _____
   _____
7. Briefly list the program's objectives. Are they clearly stated in the program or
   in the documentation? Are they educationally valuable? Are they achieved?
   _____
   _____
   _____
8. Briefly describe the program. Mention any special strengths or weaknesses.
   _____
   _____
   _____
   _____

OCTOBER · 47

Figure 7.4   Electronic Learning Review Form

Copyright © 1984 by Scholastic, Inc. Reprinted by permission of Scholastic, Inc.

PART 2
Evaluation Checklist

Please check Yes, No, or Not Applicable for each question below. To add information, or to clarify an answer, use "Comments" at the end of each section.

Yes	No	N/A	EDUCATIONAL CONTENT
___	___	___	1. Is the program content accurate?
___	___	___	2. Is the program content appropriate for intended users?
___	___	___	3. Is the difficulty level consistent for material, interest, and vocabulary?
___	___	___	4. Is the program content free of racial, sexual, or political bias?

Comments: _____

Yes	No	N/A	PRESENTATION
___	___	___	1. Is the program free of technical problems?
___	___	___	2. Are the instructions clear?
___	___	___	3. Is the curriculum material logically presented and well organized?
___	___	___	4. Do graphics, sound, and color, if used, enhance the instructional presentation?
___	___	___	5. Is the frame display clear and easy to read?

Comments: _____

Yes	No	N/A	INTERACTION
___	___	___	1. Is the feedback effective and appropriate?
___	___	___	2. Do cues and prompts help students to answer questions correctly?
___	___	___	3. Can students access the program "menu" for help or to change activities?
___	___	___	4. Can students control the pace and sequence of the program?
___	___	___	5. Are there safeguards against students "bombing" the program by erroneous inputs?

Comments: _____

Yes	No	N/A	TEACHER USE
___	___	___	1. Is record-keeping possible (within the program or through documentation worksheets)?
___	___	___	2. Does teacher have to monitor student use?
___	___	___	3. Can teacher modify the program?
___	___	___	4. Is the documentation clear and comprehensive?

Comments: _____

PART 3
Overall Evaluation
CHECK ONE.
___ Excellent program. Recommend without hesitation.
___ Pretty good program. Consider purchase.
___ Fair. But might want to wait for something better.
___ Not useful. Do not recommend purchase.

Figure 7.4 *(continued)*

approach to the problem of reviewing software is for each district to select a few teachers who will be responsible for such reviewing. One teacher might, for example, have the responsibility for reviewing language arts software for the primary grades, while another teacher might have the responsibility for reviewing social studies software for the intermediate grades. Of course, in order to discharge this responsibility adequately in a district that is serious about using computers for instruction, these teachers should receive released time from their other duties to do the reviewing.

KEEPING RECORDS OF THE EVALUATIONS

Regardless of how the evaluations of instructional software are obtained, schools should begin to develop files of these evaluations. It is much quicker to review three evaluations by three different teachers of a particular piece of instructional software than it is to do a fourth evaluation. On the basis of the available evaluations, a teacher might still find it necessary to spend some time with the software to be sure that it is usable, but much of the work involved in making that determination should have already been effectively done by the earlier reviewers.

Along with the local evaluations, schools' files should include copies of published evaluations of software. Many of the professional journals, both those devoted only to computer education and those devoted to the teaching of particular content areas, publish reviews of instructional software. One of the major difficulties in staying current about educational computing is that these reviews rarely are collected in one place. They remain scattered throughout many journals and are therefore essentially unavailable to many teachers. If they were regularly put in local files of evaluations, then teachers could make use of them to avoid some of the instructional software that does not appear to be of high enough quality. Some sources of collections of evaluations of software are provided in Figure 7.5.

Two other sources of evaluation information that all teachers need to be aware of are: Resources in Computer Education (RICE), an electronic data base of information about microcomputer course-

The Apple Software Directory, Volume 3, Education, WIDL
Video, 5245 W. Diversey Avenue, Chicago, IL 60639

Atari Program Exchange, Atari, Inc., P. O. Box 427, Sunnyvale,
CA 94086

The Commodore Software Encyclopedia, Commodore Corpo-
rate Offices, Education Department, 487 Devon Park Drive,
Wayne, PA 19087

Computer Courseware Reviews, available from Computer Technology Project, Alberta Education, 11160 Jasper Avenue,
Edmonton, Alberta, Canada T5K 0L2

The Digest of Software Reviews: Education, 1341 Bulldog Lane,
Suite C, Fresno, CA 93710

School Microware Directory, Dresden Associates, P. O. Box 246,
Dresden, ME 04342

Texas Instruments Program Directory, Texas Instruments, P. O.
Box 53, Lubbock, TX 79408

The TRS–80 Sourcebook and Software Directory, available
through Radio Shack stores.

Figure 7.5 Sources of collections of evaluations of software

ware, and *The Digest of Software Reviews*, a quarterly, loose-leaf publication of summaries of published reviews of instructional software.

RICE provides descriptive information about currently available
courseware for elementary and secondary schools and evaluation information on many of these packages. The descriptive information
includes the publisher, intended ability level, subject, mode of instruction, required hardware, instructional objectives, and prerequisites.
The evaluation information includes considerations of content, in-

structional quality, and technical quality. RICE was developed in part with support from the National Institute of Education, and it is accessible through the Bibliographic Retrieval Services (BRS), a national computer network. RICE can be searched by use of ERIC procedures and descriptors, as well as some other categories such as grade level, required hardware, instructional purpose, and instructional technique. Each review is a digested summary by the staff of RICE of evaluations gathered from teachers.

Gaining access to RICE does cost money; the user must pay first for access to BRS and second for access to RICE. However, the amount of time and effort saved as compared to a personal search of the literature is typically quite large. For example, a teacher could ask for a list of all the programs that could be used in grade four to teach grammar. Within a few minutes a list of all packages listed in the system would be produced. Information about any or all of the programs on the list can then be requested (Figure 7.6). As the RICE data base expands, it will become more and more useful as one tool for finding instructional packages.

The Digest of Software Reviews quarterly produces summaries of published software reviews. The summary sheet for a particular package includes much of the same descriptive information as RICE as well as summaries of published reviews of that software (Figure 7.7). A subscriber to the *Digest* must keep files of the sheets, and searching through them may eventually become time-consuming, though certainly not nearly as time-consuming as trying to search the literature for the complete reviews. The publication may be especially useful to people who do not have access to BRS, or to those who want multiple, undigested opinions on software.

One government attempt to review software and to provide collections of those reviews is the *Computer Courseware Reviews* produced by Alberta Education (the provincial department of education) in Alberta, Canada. The Computer Technology Project of Alberta Education has organized and trained teacher-reviewers in Alberta to use a courseware review scheme developed by the Project. The reviews are very strict; about 90 percent of disks reviewed fail to meet the criteria. However, the reviews provide more information about the programs than virtually any other reviewing system (Figure 7.8).

Sample RICE Printout

Suppose a teacher asked the question: "Is there an instructional package in junior high school geography which is compatible with TRS-80 software, where the program has been evaluated and found reliable?" One of the courseware packages which would be identified is "Geography Explorer: USA." If requested, RICE could provide any or all of the following information about the courseware which you choose.

Title: Geography Explorer: USA
Organization: Instant Software
Contact Information Peterborough, NH 03458
Address:
Phone Number: 800/258-5473
Contact Person: Mary Shooshan
Cost: $49.95
Hardware Type: TRS-80
System Requirements 32K, One Disk Drive, Monitor,
Hardware: Light Pen (Optional)
Software: TRSDOS or NEWDOs
Medium of Transfer: 5" Flexible Disk
Descriptors: Instruction, Elementary-Education, Intermediate-Grades, Middle-Schools, Secondary-Education, High Schools, Junior-High Schools, Social Studies, Geography
Grade Level: 4, 5, 6, 7, 8, 9, 10, 11
Mode of Instruction: Standard Instruction
Instructional Techniques: Drill and Practice, Information Retrieval
Instructional Objectives: The student will be able to identify states within regions of the U.S., and to associate state name with abbreviation, capital, largest city, nickname, population, flower and bird.

Instructional Prerequisites:

The student should know some information about the regions of the U.S., cities, states, and population.

Abstract:

Documentation Available: In Computer Program: Program Operating Instructions, Student's Instructions. In Supplementary Materials: Sample Program Output, Program Operating Instructions, Teacher's Information, Resource/Reference Information, Student Worksheets, Data, Progress Report. Content and Structure: The Package Consists of One Diskette in a 3-Ring Binder, A Teacher/Parent Guide, Sample Lesson Plans and a Lesson Plan Blank. Data Sheets of Information Contained on the Diskette and Blank Maps of the U.S. are Available for Teachers to Copy and Distribute. The Computer Presents a Menu of Three Program Sets: (1) State Name, Abbreviation, Capital, Largest City and Nickname; (2) State Area, Area Rank Population, Population Rank, Density, Density Rank, % Urban, % Urban Rank; (3) State Flower, Bird, Tree, Song and Motto. Each set presents a menu of its parts. The student is given a choice of answering by multiple choice, by given fact, or by typed-in response. The teacher can override the menu choices and the ways of responding. Potential Uses: This package can be used as a review in an elementary geography class. It can be used for drill on state names, abbreviations, relative location and state facts. Other uses could be enrichment or review for small groups. Perhaps some of the statistical ranking parts could be used in middle grades.

Evaluation of Major Strengths:

The Geography Explorer has a "teacher" mode which allows the teacher to choose the content and how the content is to be presented. This mode permits directed learning. Easy entry and friendly computer responses help the elementary student. A variety of graphic rewards provide immediate positive reinforcement. Student scores can be displayed.

Major Weaknesses:

Recommended audience age is too young for much of the program content. Elementary students have trouble with most of the content of the Set II: State's Area, Population, Density and Percent Urban. The graphics are not always clear, making it hard to define the shapes of states. Largest city, (Set I, Part 4) only lists the one city of the state. The other two choices are outside the state. Thus, a student only needs to relate the city to the state to answer the largest city problem.

Site and Date:

January 1982, by staff members of West Lafayette School Corporation, West Lafayette, Indiana, with the support of Indiana Title IVC.

Evaluation Summary:

Key: SA = Strongly Agree; A = Agree; D = Disagree; SD = Strongly Disagree; NA = Not Applicable

Summary of Results:

Content Accuracy (SA); Educational Value (A); Lacks Cultural Stereotyping (A); Objectives Well-Defined (D); Accomplishes State Objectives (D); Clarity of Content Presentation (A); Appropriate Difficulty Level (A); Appropriate Graphics/Sound/Color (A); Appropriate Motivational Level (A); Challenges Student Creativity (D); Feedback Effectively Employed (A); Student Controls Presentation of Format (A); Appropriate Integration with Prior Learning (D); Content Can Be Generalized (A); Program Comprehensiveness (SA); Adequate Packaging (A); Effective Information Displays (D); Clarity of Instructions (A); Teacher Facility With Program (SA); Appropriate Use of Computer Technology (A); Program Reliability (A).

Recommendation:

Evaluators indicate they would use or recommend use of package with little or no change. Refer to Evaluator's Guide ED 206 330 for interpretation of evaluative criteria.

Figure 7.6   RICE printout

Source: Northwest Regional Educational Laboratory.

The Digest of
SOFTWARE REVIEWS
Education

ERNIE'S QUIZ

DISKETTE TITLE: Ernie's Quiz

AUTHOR: Children's Television Workshop

PRODUCER: Apple Computer, Inc.
20525 Mariani Avenue
Cupertino, CA 95014

COPYRIGHT: 1982

PRICE: $50.00

SYSTEM REQUIREMENTS: Apple II, II+ or IIe/48K/disk drive/game paddles/color monitor

CONTENTS: 1 diskette, 1 back-up diskette, Activity booklet

PUBLISHER'S SUGGESTED
GRADE LEVEL: Ages 4 - 7

SUGGESTED GROUP SIZE: Individual or small group

INSTRUCTIONAL MODE: Educational game, Creative activity

DEWEY DECIMAL
CLASSIFICATION NUMBER: 793.7

SEARS SUBJECT
HEADINGS: Puzzles, Number game

ERIC DESCRIPTORS: Puzzles, Numbers

PUBLISHER'S DESCRIPTION: "ERNIE'S QUIZ will captivate little audiences with clever, familiar Muppets, jelly beans that stack up with fanfare, and faces your child creates using paddle controls. Everything is designed to attract and rivet attention. Guess Who--Who's that appearing on your screen? It could be Bert, Cookie Monster, Big Bird, Grover, Oscar, the Count, Barkley or Snuffy. Jelly Beans--Watch colorful jelly beans pile up in a jar. Count them and enter your answer. Face It--Create a face. Make it happy, sad or funny. Ernie's Quiz-- Guess Which Muppet is blue and furry? Who eats chocolate chip things? Surprises include tricks by Ernie and Cookie Monster."

COMPUTE! February 1983
"I have received several new excellent programs for young children...the CTW versions are especially well designed, easy to use, and contain fine graphics...for children four to seven years old...colorful, low-resolution pictures of Sesame Street Muppets...an excellent and varied set of software for introducing young children to computers." Glenn M. Kleiman, p. 116

THE COMPUTING TEACHER May 1983
"...four easy-to-enter, well-documented and colorful game-like activities designed to gently cajole four to seven year olds into recognizing patterns, counting, constructing modular designs and making informed guesses...requires some adult help or confident reading and typing on the part of the child. The five and seven year olds I observed...enjoyed discovering their parts in the games as well as getting better at playing them. Both sound and graphics pleased the youngsters... The reservation I have about these games is their reliance on printed sentence directions for non-readers and perhaps, as mentioned before, the question of how long children may play with this software before growing tired of it." David Ouellette, pp. 22-23

INFOWORLD July 11, 1983
"One of the things that impressed me most about ERNIE'S QUIZ was the fact that in addition to the four games in the program itself, the documentation included follow-up activities for practicing the same skills that are needed in the games...your child is discovering and practicing basic concepts needed for learning...requires adult assistance the first couple of times... The on-screen documentation is in large, uppercase letters, making it easy for a child who can read to follow them. Everything about ERNIE'S QUIZ from Apple indicates the thought and care that went into its creation. It is appropriate for the age level at which it is aimed and well done in every respect." Patti Littlefield, pp. 46-47

February 1984
Vol. 2 No. 1

Figure 7.7 Digest Review

Reprinted by permission.

POPULAR COMPUTING August 1983
"In the new Discovery software, no one or nothing gets exploded, eaten, or otherwise destroyed...(and) the children I observed playing these games seemed as enthralled and delighted as their counterparts who pop off aliens...in the instruction booklets are a number of related games and simple activities to do without a computer... The title game, ERNIE'S QUIZ, is the star of the set--at least for the children I tested it with... With this age group (4 to 7), we found it important to have an older child or adult to help with the reading and typing... These small criticisms notwithstanding, my hat is off to Children's Television Workshop for designing these games and to Apple Computer for marketing them. May there be many more to come." John O. Green, pp. 200-203

SOFTALK February 1983
"One of the strongest points of the package is its stress on the positive...child is never told that the response typed is wrong, only that the computer's answer isn't the same...can be played by kids of ages four to seven without the aid of an adult... Each game on the disk is supplemented by descriptions of two or three games that don't require a computer." Jean Varven, pp. 100-101

SOFTWARE REPORTS July 1983
"Exercises problem-solving and recall ability, stimulates creativity and acquaints children with computers. Excellent use of color graphics... Grade: B+." p. ME-4

Figure 7.7 *(continued)*

GERTRUDE'S SECRETS

DESCRIPTION

Disk Title: Gertrude's Secrets
Producer: The Learning Company
Address: 545 Middlefield Road, Suite 170, Menlo Park,California, 94025
Users :   Ages 4-9
Contents: 1 disk, 1 User's Manual (8p), Activity Cards
Topics: Problem solving
Additional Hardware/Software Requirements: Color Monitor, joystick optional
Other Formats Available (not evaluated): Available in Apple format only

Version: 1982
Cost: $44.95 U.S.
Tel. #: (415) 328-5410
Subject: Mathematics
Format: Apple II+, IIe

OBJECTIVES

This disk is intended to motivate students in their acquisition of manipulative skills and in color and shape recognition. They will learn how to create order and to plan ahead by solving puzzles that involve arranging game pieces according to a given rule or by guessing a secret rule.

CONTENT DESCRIPTION

This program consists of three types of puzzles, each having two or three levels of difficulty. The child manipulates colored shapes to solve problems involving similarities and differences. Two of the puzzles require the student to arrange shapes according to given rules. The third puzzle requires the student to decide what rule is being applied (intersection of sets). The program includes seven rule pages giving instructions for each puzzle, five sample pages showing what a correctly completed puzzle looks like, a branch allowing for the selection of different shapes with which to play, an editing feature whereby new shapes can be created by the teacher or learner and an optional tutorial. There is also a small student manual to aid in learning the basic operating procedures and a set of 16 cards that can be colored and used to play one of the three games that are suggested on the two activity cards.

CONTENT EVALUATION

The content is appropriate and effective in its sequence and is accurate, clear and unbiased. The range and depth are most appropriate for grade 1 and early grade 2 students. The upper end of the target audience (8-9 year olds) will likely find most of the puzzles too easy.

INSTRUCTIONAL FORMAT DESCRIPTION

Student interaction consists of using a joystick or set of keys to move a graphic character (Gertrude the Goose), a rectangle (representing the learner), and various game pieces (colored shapes) around the screen. By moving the goose and the rectangle through various "doors", the student selects the puzzle to be played and may opt to see a set of printed instructions, a completed sample puzzle, choose the game pieces with which to play, or alter existing pieces to create new shapes.

When a puzzle has been solved, positive feedback consists of the lines surrounding the puzzle flashing and Gertrude delivering a "treasure" to the "treasure room". A solution is never evaluated as being incorrect. Until a puzzle is accurately solved, the program considers it to be in the process of being solved.

There are some clues available to aid the player who is having difficulty solving a puzzle. In two of the puzzle types, incorrectly placed pieces will "fall out" of the puzzle.

Figure 7.8 Alberta Education Review

IMPACT OF ILLEGAL COPYING

A discussion of evaluating instructional software would not be complete without giving some attention to the impact of illegal copying on the availability of review copies of such software. When schools begin the process of choosing a textbook for adoption, publishers are quite willing to send a review copy of that text to the selection committee for examination. The publishers know that no school would

INSTRUCTIONAL FORMAT EVALUATION

This is a good program for the development of problem solving strategies in young students. Since the program recognizes different possible solutions, it encourages student creativity and enables re-solving the puzzles a number of times without loss of motivation. The instructional technique, student interaction, and evaluation techniques are appropriate and effective. However, the feedback techniques are lacking in that the program has only a few provisions for aiding the student who is having difficulty solving a puzzle or understanding instructions.

The shapes editing feature is time consuming and unnecessary. Students would enjoy creating new shapes but these are not necessary for the development of problem solving abilities, and all created shapes are lost when the computer is turned off.

It is unfortunate that the program doesn't include a management system to keep track of students' names, types of puzzle played and the number of puzzles solved.

TECHNICAL DESIGN DESCRIPTION

Graphics and color are employed in the design of the map, the puzzle, Gertrude the Goose, the shapes used for playing and the treasures won. Sound, which is at the user's control, occurs in the title page (a brief tune), when pieces are picked up or dropped (a beep), and when a puzzle has been solved (a tune).

TECHNICAL DESIGN EVALUATION

On the whole, color, graphics and sound are appropriate and effective, however, there are a few problems. Although the displays are clear and well laid out, the vocabulary may be too difficult for young, first-time users. It is easy to accidentally slip out of the page being used and into another, but movement back in is accomplished with little effort. Some of the "doors" through which the student must move are not clearly labelled and so the student must either refer to the map in the student manual or learn through trial and error.

Generally teachers must be prepared to provide help for first-time users and younger students.

SUMMARY STATEMENT

These puzzles with their motivating technical design and thought provoking puzzles are particularly suited to the development of problem solving skills in the middle target audience range. The lack of strategy suggestions for students experiencing difficulty is the chief weakness and teacher assistance will be required.

STATUS

GERTRUDE'S SECRETS has been designated as a SUPPLEMENTARY learning resource.

PURCHASE INFORMATION

This disk may be purchased for $44.95 (U.S.) (Oct. 1983) from The Learning Company at the address given at the beginning of the report. It may also be purchased from S.E.S. Distributing Inc., 366 Adelaide Street East, Toronto, Ontario, M5A 3X9, (416)-366-4242. There, the price of an individual disk is $55.95 (Oct. 1983). Schools receive a discount of 5% (for orders less than $100), 10% ($100-$1000) or 15% (greater than $1000). Local dealers may also market the product.

Defective disks will be replaced without charge within a 90 day warranty period.

Disks which are damaged by the user will be replaced for $10 U.S. upon return of the diskette to The Learning Company (distributors may not necessarily honor this warranty). This includes disks which wear out through normal wear and tear. There is no time limit for this warranty.

Teachers will appreciate the fact that the entire program is loaded during the initial boot which allows a single disk to be used in a number of computers.

Figure 7.8 (*continued*)

ever consider making photocopies of that text for use in their classrooms, partly because the cost of photocopying the text is usually greater than the cost of buying it outright, and the quality of the reproduction is usually considerably less than the quality of the printed version. The publishers view their cooperation as a small investment necessary for the text to be considered for adoption.

However, in the domain of instructional software these considerations are not the same. Most instructional software is "copy protected" so that simple means of trying to make a duplicate of the disk will not work. However, there are commercial programs designed to break into protected software, and if they don't work, some students are eager to accept the challenge of trying to break the protection scheme. Producers of instructional software are certainly aware of both of these options, and, as a result, many are quite reluctant to send out instructional software for preview. They fear that illegal copies of the disk might be made, even though it is very clear that copying software sent out for previewing is illegal.

In part, the temptation to copy software illegally is generated by the fact that most instructional software costs in the range of $30 to $70 per disk, and the cost of a blank disk is usually less than three dollars. Thus, there is a potential "savings" of many tens of dollars per copy per disk. The apparent saving is artificial, however, for many producers have markedly increased their prices to compensate for the illegal copies that might be made from each copy that is legally sold.

At the time of the writing of this book several suits are pending before the U.S. and Canadian federal courts on how the respective copyright acts might apply to software. Until those suits are settled, it is impossible to say for sure what copying is legal and what copying is illegal. Schools should probably take a very conservative stand on the issue, however, in order to protect themselves. Teachers and students should not be allowed to use school equipment to do any kind of illegal copying. Schools must monitor the development of the legal precedents related to copying of computer disks and adjust their positions accordingly as precedents are set.

CONCLUSION

Because of the time required to preview software, it is more important for teachers to have access to evaluations of software than access to evaluations of other kinds of instructional materials. Teachers are more likely to use software that they have initial confidence in, so it would be to the advantage of software producers, schools, and teachers to begin to cooperate on building collections of software reviews. Careful evaluations would also have impact on improving the quality of software; learning would be the primary beneficiary of this.

Problem Solving and Programming

8

The introduction of microcomputers into elementary school classrooms has already caused educators to rethink many of the objectives of classroom instruction. The capabilities of microcomputers allow teachers to do things such as word processing that are not possible without these machines. One of the consequences of this rethinking is that there may be a shift in the focus of some traditional instruction from the products of learning to the processes of learning. Such a shift, however, is not certain, and if it is to be a positive change, many people are going to have to put much effort into it.

For example, in language arts instruction traditionally the strong emphasis has been on skills like grammar and spelling. The availability of word-processing programs, with accompanying programs to check spelling and grammar, decreases the need to make students proficient at these skills and correspondingly increases the need to help students learn how to put their thoughts on paper (or, in this case, on the monitor screen). Editing skills become more important. Students can easily edit with these programs, without the drudgery of having to recopy their work. The nature of communication, rather than the details of putting words on paper, may become the focus of language arts instruction. Teachers will be faced with making decisions as to how far students must go in learning technique in order to be able to communicate.

Another example is the teaching of computational algorithms in arithmetic. One of the reasons that so much attention has been given to teaching things like the long-division algorithm is that symbolic manipulation has historically been very important to students who need to study or use mathematics. However, now computer programs such as MuMath will do virtually all of the symbolic manipulation that has been taught in high school algebra and even college calculus. This "symbol pushing" has thus, at least theoretically, been reduced to the level of a "calculator" activity, just like most computation typical of elementary school arithmetic. Teachers can now focus on teaching understanding behind the manipulations rather than the manipulations themselves. But an unanswered question is how to determine the level of expertise a person needs with manipulations in order to understand a skill. No one at this point knows the answer.

In spite of the potential shift in the focus of teaching, it would be wrong to say that the introduction of computers in the schools has caused this shift. The notion of teaching for understanding goes back at least as far as the 1920s and 1930s. Brownell (1935, 1947) is recognized as one of the first to put strong emphasis on understanding as opposed to manipulative skill in arithmetic. Periodically since then, this call for understanding has reappeared in a variety of guises. Recently, for example, there has been an increasing call for emphasis on problem solving in the mathematics curriculum. In 1980 the National Council of Teachers of Mathematics published the *Agenda for Action* (NCTM, 1980) which called for problem solving to be the focus of the mathematics curriculum in the 1980s. The writing of the AGENDA was mostly completed prior to 1979, which was prior to the general availability of microcomputers, so the authors clearly did not view problem solving as inexplicably tied to the use of microcomputers. Indeed, the AGENDA contains relatively few recommendations regarding the use of microcomputers. Rather, the authors focused on underlying processes as more important than manipulation skills.

Now the availability of microcomputers and the corresponding availability of new capabilities (such as word processing and science and social studies simulations) has led other groups, like the National Council of Teachers of English, also to focus attention on processes rather than products. For example, there are now microcomputer programs that let the user create stories by responding to situations. The choices that are made determine the outcome of the stories, and creativity in choice-making can become the object of instruction. Teachers can focus students' attention on questions of "What would happen if . . . " and can let students find out some of the consequences of their decisions. Such activities can provide settings for creative writing and for stimulation of students' imaginations.

Science or social studies simulations also provide similar settings for looking at consequences of decisions. They can help teachers focus students' attention on ways in which different processes affect situations. The means to ends become the focus of instruction rather than just the ends themselves.

All such activities can be roughly classed as "problem solving"; that is, in all these activities, the focus is on the effects of decisions. Although problem solving has become especially important in discussions of the mathematics curriculum, there are also lots of opportunities for problem-solving processes to be used and studied in other content areas. One of the consequences of the potential increased focus on these processes may be the development of more interdisciplinary activities across content areas. That is, the goals of instruction may become somewhat more coherent across disciplines.

WHAT IS PROBLEM SOLVING?

One of the difficulties in discussing problem solving is that there is relatively little agreement about a specific definition of the term. For our purposes, problem solving can be characterized as a process that will allow attainment of a specified goal when there is no known algorithm for reaching that goal. For example, if the goal is to explain how a bill is passed into law in Canada, then problem solving occurs in the gathering and synthesizing of the information needed to make that explanation. Decisions will have to be made about which books to read, which people to ask, which information to remember, which information to forget, and how to organize the information. No one of these decisions alone is sufficient, and no known algorithm specifies the steps to follow in constructing the explanation.

This characterization of problem solving stands in contrast to the notion of an algorithm. An algorithm is a step-by-step procedure that, if followed correctly, will produce a specified outcome. For example, a recipe in a cookbook is a loose kind of algorithm; it provides the steps to follow in producing the dish described. Many tasks in our lives can be completed by using algorithms. Other tasks are encountered so infrequently or are so poorly understood that there are no algorithms readily available that can be employed. Problem-solving experience tends to give people confidence that they can meet these unusual tasks and figure out ways to complete them, though the solutions may not be the most efficient ones.

Problem solving is different from solving problems. For many people, solving problems occurs when a teacher assigns a set of problems (or exercises) that are highly structured to fit whatever topic is under discussion. The structured nature of these "problems" generally reduces them to exercises; typically, students have a pretty clear idea of what is to be done to produce the answers. As such, these activities usually do not constitute problem solving.

Many heuristics have been identified for problem solving; e.g., find a simpler problem, draw a picture, gather data, and look for a similar problem for which a solution is known. Most of these techniques are traceable to Polya (1973), though in spite of their relatively long history teachers are still searching for ways to incorporate them into the elementary school curriculum. It is known both that teaching and learning problem solving are difficult goals to achieve and that the advent of microcomputers opens truly new ways for working toward these goals. The task now is to use the new tool effectively.

PROBLEM SOLVING ON
MICROCOMPUTERS

The notions of problem solving, as applied to a computer environment, can be seen best in programming activities and in special computer-assisted instruction programs designed to aid in the development of problem-solving techniques. Almost everyone will agree that when students are asked to write a working program that will accomplish a specific goal (for example, a program to generate poetry), they are involved in problem solving. The design of the program, the writing of the code, the debugging of that code, and the testing of the program with sample data are all activities for which there is no known algorithm designed to produce the end result. In fact, there are many solutions for each problem, and choosing among them is itself no easy task.

There may, however, be simpler programming tasks that also involve students in problem solving. For example, students might be asked to modify an existing program to do a slightly different task. If the new task is very similar, then this activity might become an exercise. If, however, the task were more substantially different, then it would surely be problem solving. Students would have to make decisions about what part(s) of the program to alter and choose among the possible ways of making the alteration(s).

For example, the following program, which prints a pattern, could be altered to print a box (little transfer required) or to print a triangle (greater transfer required).

```
10 PRINT "*********"
20 PRINT "* *******"
30 PRINT "*    *****"
40 PRINT "*      ***"
50 PRINT "* * * * *"
60 PRINT "*      ***"
70 PRINT "*    *****"
80 PRINT "* *******"
90 PRINT "*********"
```

Trap and Guess

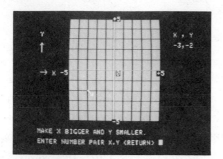

Hidden Treasure

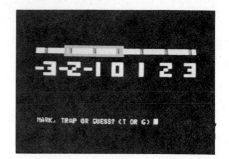

Roadblock

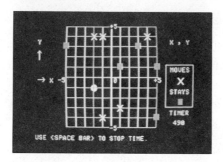

Figure 8.1   Bumble Plot programs

From *Bumbleplot Manual*, pages 16–17.

Some microcomputer software packages are designed to teach specific aspects of problem solving. These include Bumble Plot (Figure 8.1), Gertrude's Puzzles, Rocky's Boots, Mind Puzzles (Figures 8.2 to 8.4), and others. Whether these programs are truly effective at teaching problem solving is open to question right now. It would be of considerable benefit to know the kinds of students that seem to benefit from using them.

Somewhat more removed from these programs are the general tool programs that may also enhance problem-solving skills. For instance, word-processing programs can be used to improve students'

Optional Instruction frames describe the Queen Bee of Menta ritual (Figures 1-2).

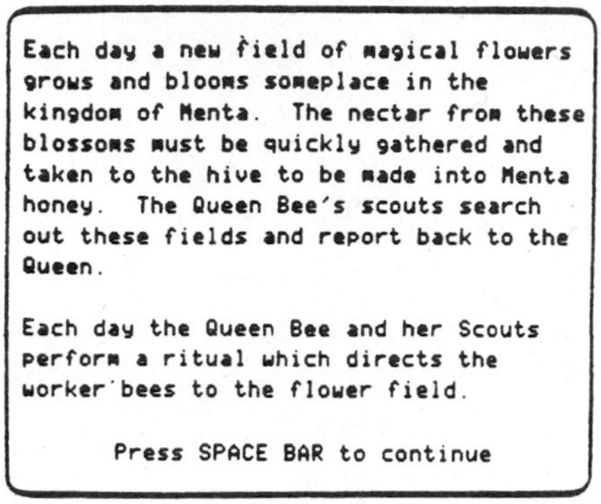

Each day a new field of magical flowers
grows and blooms someplace in the
kingdom of Menta. The nectar from these
blossoms must be quickly gathered and
taken to the hive to be made into Menta
honey. The Queen Bee's scouts search
out these fields and report back to the
Queen.

Each day the Queen Bee and her Scouts
perform a ritual which directs the
worker bees to the flower field.

Press SPACE BAR to continue

Figure 1

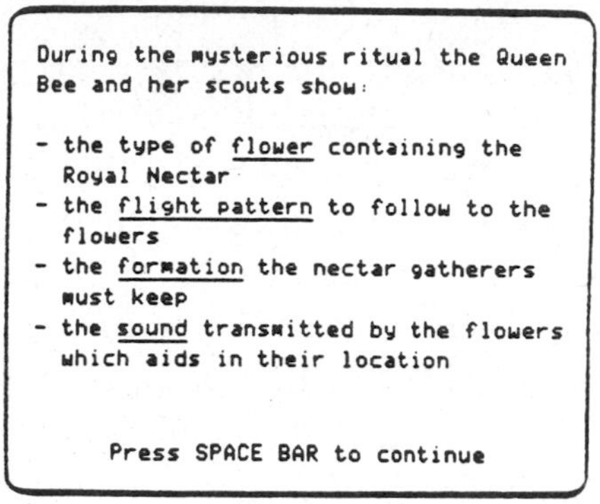

During the mysterious ritual the Queen
Bee and her scouts show:

- the type of <u>flower</u> containing the
  Royal Nectar
- the <u>flight pattern</u> to follow to the
  flowers
- the <u>formation</u> the nectar gatherers
  must keep
- the <u>sound</u> transmitted by the flowers
  which aids in their location

Press SPACE BAR to continue

Figure 2

Problem-solving strategies which will help solve the puzzle are listed and summarized (Figures 3-4).

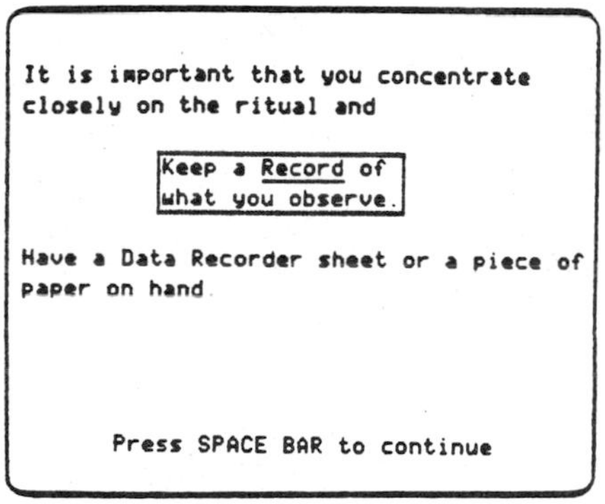

It is important that you concentrate
closely on the ritual and

Keep a <u>Record</u> of
what you observe.

Have a Data Recorder sheet or a piece of
paper on hand.

Press SPACE BAR to continue

Figure 3

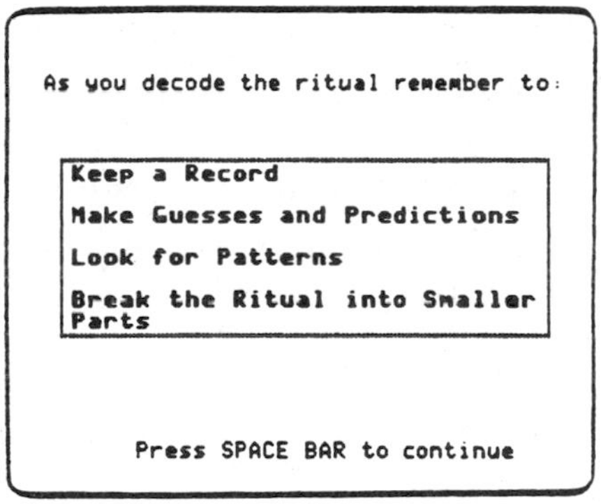

As you decode the ritual remember to:

Keep a Record

Make Guesses and Predictions

Look for Patterns

Break the Ritual into Smaller
Parts

Press SPACE BAR to continue

Figure 4

Figure 8.2   Instructions

From MECC, *Mind Puzzles*, page 26.

imaginations by having students engage in creative writing activities. Science or social studies simulations could be used to teach students how to search through information to find the particular pieces needed to solve a problem. As pointed out earlier, this requires problem-solving skills.

COMPUTER LANGUAGES FOR
PROBLEM SOLVING

There are many computer languages—BASIC, LOGO, FORTRAN, COBOL, PASCAL, ADA, C. Each language has its own strengths and weaknesses, and selecting from among them is not an easy task. Fortunately, at the elementary school level there are many fewer choices. If a computing language is taught from the standpoint of teaching general concepts for solving problems, however, one language probably does not have much advantage over another. Some languages lend themselves more easily to this kind of generality, but probably any of them could be used in this way.

BASIC (Beginner's All-purpose Symbolic Instruction Code) is the language that is built in to most microcomputers. Beware, however; each machine has a slightly different dialect of BASIC. There are many commonalities, but also some important differences. BASIC is most easily used to solve computational types of problems. Although it is not specifically a mathematics language, it lends itself easily to mathematics-oriented problems.

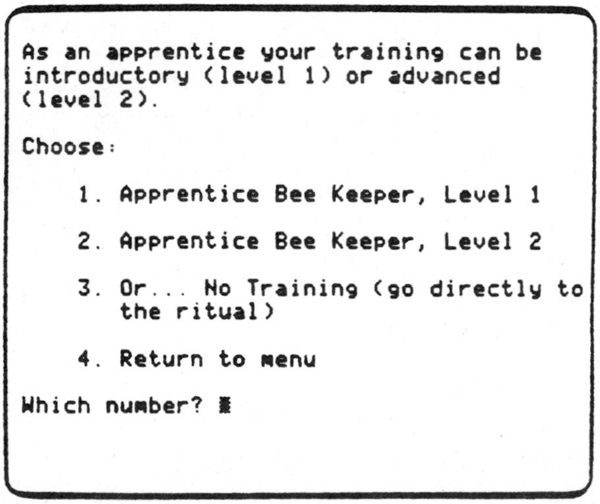

```
As an apprentice your training can be
introductory (level 1) or advanced
(level 2).

Choose:

     1. Apprentice Bee Keeper, Level 1

     2. Apprentice Bee Keeper, Level 2

     3. Or... No Training (go directly to
        the ritual)

     4. Return to menu

Which number? █
```

Figure 1

Figure 8.3   Skill levels and objectives

From MECC, *Mind Puzzles*, pages 29–30.

PROBLEM-SOLVING STRATEGY/SKILL		TASK	OPTION NUMBER
Visual Memory	•	Students remember visual data in the form of patterns, movements, and symbols.	1-3
Auditory Memory	•	Students remember auditory patterns.	1-3
Rule Application	•	Students discover and use a rule for decoding a puzzle.	3
Identifying Attributes	•	Characteristics are assigned to symbols.	1-3
Decision Making	•	Based on exploration of the programs, students decide what the code is.	1-3
Using a Model	•	A model is developed in Options 1 and 2 which must be applied in the third program.	3
Looking for Sequence	•	The sequence of events in a display is an important part of the code.	2-3
Examining Assumptions	•	Two programs allow students to use the computer to test out their assumptions.	2-3
Seeing Cause and Effect	•	Students create displays which they think will result in a certain predicted display.	2-3
Revising a Guess	•	Exploring these programs by the guess-and-revise method is a successful strategy.	1-3
Use of Symbol	•	Symbols represent sequences of events in a display.	1-3
Dividing a Problem into Less Complex Parts	•	The most successful solution to the puzzle requires use of this strategy.	3
Using Charts and Tables	• •	Charts are created. Charts and records are used to solve the problem.	1 2-3
Predicting	•	Programs allow students to predict the symbols and the order of symbols for duplicating displays.	2-3
Labeling	• •	Use of the record section of the work screen. Creation of their own records.	2-3
Making Choices	•	Choose between many possible symbols and orders of symbols.	1-3
Looking for Pattern	•	Patterns of displays and symbols are determined by students.	2-3
Risk Taking	•	Students have the option of guessing on the chance of attaining a higher score.	3

Figure 2

Figure 8.3 (continued)

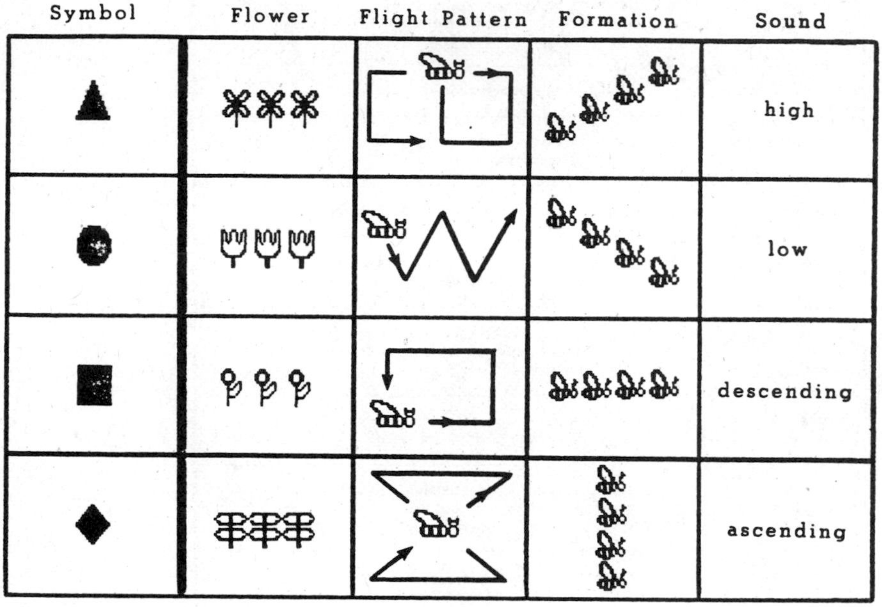

Symbol	Flower	Flight Pattern	Formation	Sound
▲	✳✳✳			high
⬤	♈♈♈			low
■	♀♀♀			descending
♦	⚏⚏⚏			ascending

Figure 3

Figure 8.4   Key to the Ritual

From MECC, *Mind Puzzles*, page 31.

Two sample BASIC programs follow. The first program computes the average of numbers that are entered via the keyboard; the first information the program requests is the number of numbers that are to be averaged. The second program generates all the prime numbers less than 100.

```
10 PRINT "THIS PROGRAM COMPUTES THE AVERAGE OF
NUMBERS YOU ENTER."
20 INPUT "HOW MANY NUMBERS DO YOU WANT TO
AVERAGE";N
30 FOR I = 1 TO N
40 INPUT A
50 S = S + A: REM S IS THE RUNNING TOTAL OF
THE NUMBERS
60 NEXT I
70 PRINT "THE AVERAGE OF YOUR ";N;" NUMBERS
IS ";S/N
80 END
```

```
10 PRINT "THIS PROGRAM WILL PRINT ALL PRIMES
   LESS THAN 100."
20 PRINT "THE FIRST PRIME IS 2."
30 PRINT "THE OTHER PRIMES ARE ";
40 FOR I = 3 TO 100
50 FOR J = 2 TO I-1
60 IF INT(I/J) = I/J THEN GOTO 90
70 NEXT J
80 PRINT I;" ";
90 NEXT I
100 PRINT
```

LOGO, a language developed at Massachusetts Institute of Technology especially for young children, has had a lot of "good press" as an environment in which children can learn to solve problems by being in command of their own world. The notion of a LOGO environment may be critical. Partial implementations of the language may be inadequate. The research now beginning to be completed does not seem to show any overwhelming advantage for LOGO, nor does it show any great disadvantage in using LOGO, as opposed to other instructional techniques for teaching problem solving. LOGO does seem quite well suited for approaching problems from a group-task perspective, so if cooperation is one skill that is deemed important, then LOGO might be an ideal choice. It is an "add-on" for almost every microcomputer system, however, and the cost of implementing it may discourage some people.

Two sample LOGO graphics programs follow. The first program draws a triangle, and the second spins that triangle to create a design.

```
TO TRIANGLE
  FORWARD 100
  LEFT 120
  FORWARD 100
  LEFT 120
  FORWARD 100
  LEFT 120
END
```

```
TO SPINTRIANGLE
 REPEAT 6   [ TRIANGLE RIGHT 60 ]
END
```

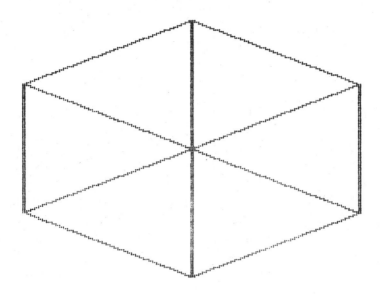

PROGRAMMING IN THE
PRIMARY GRADES

The use of BASIC generally requires some minimal mathematics background such as knowledge of the mathematical operations. Shumway (1984) has provided some examples of ways that primary teachers might get started through demonstrations of writing programs. This approach requires only one machine with a monitor in a position that can be seen by the children. One sample program that might be used is the following:

```
10 FOR K = 1 TO 10
20 PRINT K, K+1, K+2
30 NEXT K
```

This program will print triples of successive numbers:

```
1    2    3
2    3    4
3    4    5
4    5    6
5    6    7
6    7    8
7    8    9
8    9    10
9    10   11
10   11   12
```

Several patterns can be noticed by the children. First, in each column, the numbers increase successively. Second, there are diagonals of the same numbers. Third, the formatting of the computer in columns does not keep the ones digits lined up, as is required in many school mathematics tasks. This observation is important because it points out one of the changes (i.e., less emphasis on lining up digits) that may have to take place in the mathematics curriculum as computers become more and more common in elementary school.

After a sample program like this is presented, it is fairly easy to begin to make modifications in the program. For example, line 20 might be changed to the following:

```
20 PRINT K, K+2, K+4
```

Students can be asked to predict what changes might occur in the output of the program. Another change is the following:

```
20 PRINT K, K+K, K+K+K
```

This change causes some significant changes in the patterns of the output, and it might be a convenient way to introduce the topic of repeated addition, which could in turn lead to investigation of multiplication.

Students can also investigate simple designs with BASIC. For example, the following program prints out a pattern:

```
10 PRINT "**********"
20 PRINT "*        *"
30 PRINT "*        *"
40 PRINT "*        *"
50 PRINT "*        *"
60 PRINT "*        *"
70 PRINT "**********"
```

Alterations of the pattern (e.g., elongation of the rectangle) can be generated by inserting lines like the following:

```
25 PRINT "*        *"
```

Students might also be challenged to produce a rectangle with one of the diagonals drawn inside it.

Many projects are within the reach of primary-grade students through the use of LOGO's turtle graphics capability. Papert (1980) discusses typical projects developed by quite young students. One of the first is to have students draw a square.

```
FD 50
RT 90
FD 50
RT 90
FD 50
RT 90
FD 50
```

Whether one wants to add an additional line (RT 90) so that the turtle is pointing in the same direction at the end as at the beginning of the drawing is a question more of convenience and of style than of substance in learning about problem solving. This program can be shortened by use of the REPEAT command, and it can be made into a procedure by using the command TO.

```
TO SQUARE
  REPEAT 4 [FD 50 RT 90]
END
```

Now the drawing of a square can be completed simply by calling on this newly defined procedure in any other program.

```
SQUARE
FD 50
SQUARE
```

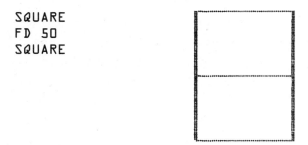

This program will draw two squares, one directly above the other. More complicated designs could be imagined by orienting the turtle in various ways before drawing copies of the square.

```
SQUARE
LT 45
SQUARE
```

Other projects that students seem to enjoy completing with LOGO are drawing a house, a head, or a city skyline. Many young students become quite involved with LOGO and spend a lot of time working on their projects. A single project can be broken down into pieces, and the pieces can be shared by all the students in a group. In this way, cooperation skills can be practiced along with the programming skills.

Delta Draw is one of several other kinds of drawing programs. Students can create designs by using built-in shapes (e.g., squares, circles, triangles) and built-in coloring routines (e.g., color the inside of a circle green). These programs are quite easy to use and could become an integral part of the art curriculum in an elementary school. Too, creating designs could be used to supplement a creative writing curriculum by giving students opportunities to be creative in multiple modes—writing and drawing—simultaneously.

PROGRAMMING IN THE INTERMEDIATE GRADES

As students' mathematics backgrounds increase, BASIC can be integrated in the curriculum in many more ways. In part this is due to the wider range of mathematics and mathematics-oriented content that is included in the intermediate grades, but it is also due in part to the students' greater sophistication at dealing with variables. The following program will generate nonsense verse.

```
10 FOR K = 1 TO 2
20 READ A$(K)
30 NEXT K
40 DATA SEVILLE,QUADRILLE
45 :::
50 FOR J = 1 TO 2
60 READ B$(J)
70 NEXT J
80 DATA SWILL,FILL
85 :::
90 FOR I = 1 TO 2
100 READ C$(I)
110 NEXT I
120 DATA QUILLS,MILLS
125 :::
150 FOR P = 1 TO 3
160 X(P) = INT (2 * RND(9)) + 1
170 NEXT P
175 :::
200 PRINT "THE GURU OF ";A$(X(1))
210 PRINT "GAVE ALL HIS WEALTH FOR "; B$(X(2))
220 PRINT "HE THEN WENT DOWN"
230 PRINT "TO LONDON TOWN"
240 PRINT "AND ASKED THE KING FOR "; C$(X(3))
250 END
```

The computer can also be used to generate data to use in problem solving. The following program generates data to help solve the problem of finding the largest area that can be enclosed in a rectangular region with a constant perimeter of forty meters.

```
10 PRINT "LENGTH", "WIDTH", "AREA"
20 FOR K = 1 TO 20
30 PRINT K,20-K,K*(20-K)
40 NEXT K
50 END
```

The student can look through the output and find the largest integral value of the area. Then follow-up data can be generated to determine if nonintegral sides generate larger areas.

LOGO also can be expanded for intermediate-grade students. One of the best ways is to introduce "recursion" in a program. Recursion is having a procedure call itself. The following example continues to generate squares until the user intervenes by typing CTRL-G.

```
TO MULTIPLE.SQUARE
  REPEAT 4 [ FORWARD 40 RIGHT 90 ]
  FORWARD 15
  LEFT 20
  MULTIPLE.SQUARE
END
```

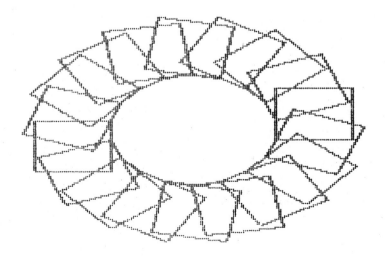

After drawing a square, moving forward fifteen steps, and turning left twenty degrees, the procedure calls itself. It then proceeds to draw another square, move forward, turn left, call itself, etc. The user must intervene in order to make the turtle stop.

A more sophisticated recursive procedure will contain a conditional statement that will determine when it is supposed to stop. The following program will draw a spiral.

```
TO SPIRAL :SIZE
  HIDETURTLE
  IF :SIZE < 2 THEN [STOP]
  FORWARD :SIZE
  LEFT 10
  SPIRAL :SIZE - 2
END
```

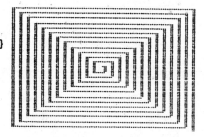

Recursion is a very powerful technique in programming, and much experience working with it is required to begin to develop a firm understanding of it. Early exposure to simple instances of recursion might put students on the road to that understanding.

RESEARCH ON PROGRAMMING AND PROBLEM SOLVING

Many claims have been made about the effects of teaching programming on problem solving as well as on the cognitive organization learners create for information. Unfortunately, there is not a correspondingly large body of evidence either to support or refute these claims.

Mayer (1982) made five recommendations for teaching programming meaningfully; these were based on a variety of studies that he and his colleagues have completed.

1. Provide the learner with a concrete model of the computer.

2. Encourage the learner to actively restate the new technical information in his or her own words.
3. Assess the learner's existing intuitions about computer operation and try to build on them, or modify them, as needed.
4. Provide the learner with methods for chunking statements into a larger, single, meaningful unit.
5. Provide the learner with methods for analyzing statements into smaller, meaningful parts. (p. 129)

Although these should not be taken as verified facts about the learning and the teaching of programming, they do raise some interesting concerns about structuring teaching. Perhaps of most importance is the highlighting of the role of intuitions that students bring to learning. Many students will have had some exposure to computers or to calculators. Their personal notions will greatly color the ways in which they perceive the instruction that is provided. If the instruction is inconsistent with those notions, it is likely to be counterproductive. That is, students are not likely to assimilate the instruction well if it is counter to their own notions of computers. The first chore for a teacher, then, is to identify and perhaps to remold the students' intuitions.

A second important observation of Mayer's is that chunking information is important for programming skill. For example, if a student needs to have the program read in data from a DATA statement in BASIC, the entire FOR/NEXT loop that does this should become the object of attention rather than each individual line in the loop. Students apparently do not naturally chunk information in this way; teachers must point out the desirability of doing so.

Soloway, Lochhead, and Clement (1982) have tried to approach the question of programming and problem solving more directly, and they claim to have demonstrated that programming does enhance problem solving. Their subjects were college students, rather than elementary school students, however; and their data might better be described as demonstrating that, for some students, solving a problem is easier by writing a program in BASIC than by writing an algebraic equation. It is not clear that such results, especially based on the scanty data, have any direct implications for teaching elementary school students, but they raise the hope that the claim of transfer from programming to problem solving may eventually be verified for a wider range of students and activities.

Blume (1984) provided an updated summary of evidence on whether "programming-augmented mathematics instruction" (that is, teaching mathematics through some exposure to programming) enhanced problem-solving skills. Only one study was reported with elementary students, thus indicating the scantiness of the knowledge base in this area. In that study fifth-graders solved word problems either directly or by writing programs to help. The direct-instruction students scored higher on the posttest, but the question was raised whether the writing of the computer programs took so much time that those students simply did not have sufficient time to learn the mathematics.

A few studies have dealt with the use of LOGO in elementary school settings, but since LOGO is relatively new, there has not been time for in-depth study of its effects. Blume (1984) reported two studies in which a LOGO group outperformed a non-LOGO group in use of problem-solving heuristics on problem-solving tasks. One other single-group experiment demonstrated that LOGO students improved in their grasp of the concept *variable*. Again, these results suggest some possible effects of the use of LOGO, but they should not be considered as verified truths.

Rampy (1984) had interviewers watch fifth-graders program in LOGO over a six-week period. She noted that the students seemed to fall into two groups: process-oriented and product-oriented. The process students experimented with the LOGO commands, apparently to explore the power inherent in the commands. They often went off on tangents when an unexpected event happened. The product students, on the other hand, worked extensively in immediate execution mode in order to accomplish the task at hand. They rarely followed up on the "bugs" they encountered; rather, they focused attention on trying to correct those bugs to fit the task.

Brown and Rood (1984) taught BASIC and LOGO to different groups of gifted students in grades 2 through 9. There was no differential effect of the two languages, though collectively the groups improved in problem-solving ability. This is not too surprising, since both languages were taught with a common "guided discovery learning" approach. This points up the importance of the instructional approach and goals, rather than the importance of the internal structure of the particular language used for instruction.

Clements and Gullo (1984) compared the changes in general cognitive abilities of eighteen six-year-olds, half of whom studied LOGO and half of whom used CAI (arithmetic drill). The treatments lasted twelve weeks. The students using CAI displayed no significant change on any measure. The LOGO group scored significantly higher on the posttest than on the pretest for measures of divergent thinking and reflectivity. Some of the effect may have been due to the graphics in LOGO as compared to the arithmetic emphasis of the CAI. Too, since the CAI rewarded quick responses, it may have worked against increased reflectivity in the CAI group.

CONCLUSION

There is a lot of interest in investigating the effects of programming instruction on problem-solving abilities, either directly or indirectly through programming-augmented instruction. There appear to be some limited areas in which programming might improve problem-solving performance. However, to expect the general, and perhaps magical, transfer from programming to other areas (as claimed by Papert, 1980) is almost certainly unrealistic. Teachers must be alert to different outcomes with different kinds of students, such as are suggested by Rampy (1984). Only in this way can the learning of students be maximized.

Word Processing

9

One of the major advantages of using computers is that they are extremely fast at manipulating information. Most people who think about this capability tend to stereotype the kind of information that can be manipulated as only numeric. That stereotype is not at all accurate. Computers are just as capable of manipulating other kinds of symbolic information, such as characters or words. (Of course, the internal representation is numeric, but that need not concern the user.) That is, the computer can be turned into a processor of words just as easily as a processor of numbers.

WHAT IS WORD PROCESSING?

Word processing is the use of a machine to manipulate textual information; that is, strings of characters, whether the characters are letters, numbers, or punctuation marks. Word processing may be very simplistic, as in the case of a typewriter, or it may be very complex, as in the case of a sophisticated word-processing computer program.

In the simplest case the typewriter merely prints on paper exactly what is typed; that is, the letters on the keys that are struck. It has no built-in correcting function and cannot move words around on the page. Many people have had the experience of writing a draft of a paper then deciding that the paragraphs needed to be rearranged.

Frequently the "cut and paste" method is used to do this rearranging; the paragraphs are cut apart, rearranged, taped onto new pages, and a new version is then retyped. Those kinds of tasks, along with correcting typos, reformatting text, and adding or deleting text, can now be done electronically, either on a machine that is solely dedicated to word processing or on a computer that is equipped with a program that makes the computer act for a time as if it were dedicated solely to word processing. A word processor thus allows considerable flexibility to an author to try out words, phrases, sentences, paragraphs, or even whole chapters without having the drudgery of retyping new drafts. (Indeed, this book was written with a word-processing program, with lots of rearranging of both words and ideas.)

The first word processors were machines dedicated only to this purpose. Since a computer is a multifunction tool, it must be fooled into behaving like a word processor. A word processing program carries out this deception.

Knapp (1984) gives a good summary of the desirable functions to look for in a word-processing program. The most important are listed below:

- Text Editing Functions
  writing and editing in one mode
  replace text through both insertion/deletion and search/
      replace
  delete text by character, word, sentence, line, paragraph, or
      complete file
  insert text with automatic reformatting
  move text
  cursor movement
  recovery features to correct mistaken deletions
- Screen Display
  format text easily
  show finished document on screen
  set margins, spacing, underlining, etc.
  embedded commands to change margins, spacing, etc.
- Help Features
  menus

manuals and reference cards
tutorial program
• Compatible Programs
mail merge or form letters
spelling checker
data base management (pp. 55–56)

It must be remembered that a word processor (or a computer that believes it is a word processor) is, after all, quite dumb; it cannot interpret the sense of what the author is writing and can only manipulate the characters that are typed in. Further, these manipulations are carried out exactly according to the directions the user gives the program. This raises the question of whether typing skill is going to become essential for school children. After all, a better typist is likely to be a more efficient, though perhaps not a more accurate, word-processor user. No one at this point in the use of computers in the schools can say for sure what the role of typing skills will be. Probably as more and more children gain access to word processors, they will become motivated to learn enough typing skills to become relatively efficient users. Beyond that level of skill, however, there may be no real need to teach typing. In particular, since making corrections is so easy, great accuracy at typing does not seem necessary.

There are basically three stages to writing with a word processor. First, the draft of the work is typed into the machine, with the text appearing on the monitor instead of on paper. While this is being done, the author has the option of backspacing at any time to correct mistakes in typing or to change words or phrases. The corrections are made electronically, and there is no need, for example, to wait for the correcting fluid to dry, as typically is the case in typing. After the draft is finished, the author must tell the machine to store the words electronically on some permanent storage device, such as a computer disk. A very important lesson is always learned the first time this command is forgotten before the machine is turned off. (In such a case the work is all lost, and it must be redone.)

Second, the draft can be viewed on the screen or on a printout and corrections can be made. At this stage, material can be added or deleted or parts of the text (as small as single letters or as large as many lines) can be moved around electronically to determine their best positions. Since this is all done inside the memory of the machine, there is no need to worry about having to retype versions. For example, if a change needs to be made in the first paragraph, the machine automatically adjusts the spacing of the remainder of the work so that retyping is not necessary.

Third, once all the changes have been made, the final copy can be printed out on paper, or can be sent electronically (over telephone lines or by satellite) around the world. Even at this stage, if changes need to be made, they can be completed and a new final version can be printed.

One of the primary advantages of using a word processor is that an author does not have to settle for work that is merely acceptable simply because the task of reproducing a new version is so onerous. Rather, an author can set standards as high as desired and can work until those standards are reached. Likewise, a teacher of writing can set high standards and not be obliged to accept work that does not meet those standards just because the recopying of the work, either by hand or by typing, is difficult or time-consuming.

INSTRUCTIONAL OBJECTIVES FOR WORD PROCESSING

In the context of the elementary school curriculum, the use of word processing might significantly change the ways that writing and communication are taught. The primary goals of writing instruction seem to be to teach children correct use of spelling, grammar, and sentence construction while also helping them to learn to organize information into a coherent whole. Word processing can assist greatly in all of these tasks.

Spelling is one of the easiest things to correct with a word processor. If a mistake is made only once, the author need only call up the text, search through it until the misspelled word is found, and then retype that word. If a mistake is made with some consistency, most word processors contain a feature that allows the author to call up the text and then to have the machine itself search for each occurrence of the misspelled word and change each of those occurrences to the correct spelling. This means that teachers could refuse to accept a paper until all of the misspelled words are corrected. The child does not have to do the retyping, which is done automatically, so the time spent in making the corrections is relatively very short.

Grammar and sentence construction might also be corrected in similar ways. It might not be easy for children to know when to correct their grammar, but a paper that has been marked by the teacher can be returned to the student and a corrected version can be demanded. Again, the task of producing the new copy is very easy.

The ease with which the technical details of writing can be handled will allow both the teacher and the students to focus their attention on the organization of thoughts into a coherent whole. The focus of instruction, therefore, might turn from technical detail to logical thinking and logical expression of one's thoughts. Either the teacher or the student (or both) could set the standards for acceptable communication in a particular piece of work and revisions could be made until those standards are attained.

This means that the processes of revising writing may become more important than the processes of original organization of that work, though, of course, if the original organization is good, the amount of revision needed will be greatly reduced. Some of the time that is spent on trying to convince children to outline a paper before they begin writing, for example, may be converted into time spent on teaching children how to read their work with a critical eye and how to know when to revise and when to leave well enough alone.

Creative writing can also be made easier with the use of a word processor. An author can sit down and let her/his imagination loose. Bits and pieces of a work can be typed in with the full realization that they can be edited, moved around, deleted, or added to at any time. This allows a work to generate itself, at least partially, without the author's feeling restricted by the time needed to reproduce a copy of the work.

WORD PROCESSORS FOR THE ELEMENTARY SCHOOL

There are a variety of word processors that teachers have used successfully with elementary school students. Before one is described as a sample, some general guidelines will help to identify the features that such a word processor needs to have.

First, it should be easy to use and should require essentially no knowledge of the workings of a computer. In computer jargon this is called "user-friendly." All that a student should have to do is put the computer disk into the disk drive and turn on the machine. From that point on the student should be prompted by the program itself about what needs to be done. Of course, the student will have some choices to make, and s/he needs to know how those choices will affect the work being written. But the operation of the machine should almost always be prompted by the machine telling the user what needs to be done.

Second, the word processor should allow easy editing of the work. This includes moving text around, deleting text, adding text, and search and replace functions. (This last function means that the program itself will search for all occurrences of a particular string of characters and, if instructed to do so, replace them with another string of characters. An example of this is in changing every isolated occurrence of "i" with "I".) Some word processors also have built-in safety features; that is, when a user instructs the program to delete or move something, the program prompts the user by asking if s/he really means to do this. This is obviously not a necessary feature of word processors, but it is quite desirable, especially for use with young children.

Third, the printing commands should be easy to use. Options that ought to be part of such commands are the number of characters per line, the number of lines per page, whether pages are to be numbered and, if so, whether the numbering goes at the top or the bottom, spacing between lines, and the number of copies to be printed.

Beyond these essential features of any word processor a number of extra features make a word processor more or less useful. Carriage returns should be marked by a special character or symbol on the monitor screen (but *not* on the printed copy) so that the author knows where they are. When they appear as blank spaces on the monitor, the author has to guess whether s/he has inadvertently hit a RETURN at the end of a line on the screen when a RETURN was not intended.

These extra RETURNs do not show up until the printed copy is made. At that point it may be difficult to figure out why the printed copy is formatted in such a strange way. Adults who first learn to use a word processor typically want to hit a carriage return at the end of each line on the monitor screen, since that most closely models the behavior they have learned to use with a typewriter. However, a word processor automatically takes care of the spacing of words on the page, except at the ends of paragraphs, so novice users typically have too many carriage returns in their work.

It is also nice to have the capability to embed formatting commands (such as underlining or changes in the margins) in the text. Primarily this is done so that the printed version of the work is formatted in special ways as it is being printed. The simplest type of embedded command is indenting of pieces of text, such as might be required if a long quotation were included in the middle of a paper. Virtually all word-processing programs allow this simple capability, but sometimes only indenting on the left side is allowed. Sophisticated uses of embedding of commands would be required in the writing of poetry so that some lines are indented within the poem, or in the writing of an outline with its formal system of indentations. In writing reports, say of science laboratory assignments, it is often necessary to put in tables of information. Embedding of formatting commands is the best way to create these tables with multiple columns. A simple word-processing program may not have the capability to handle this type of task.

One of the most talked-about word processors is Bank Street Writer, developed at Bank Street College in New York. It was created for use by elementary school students who were assumed to be novice computer users. The first feature of this word processor to be noticed is that at all times the commands available to the user are displayed at the top of the screen. Once these commands are understood, the program becomes very user-friendly, since the repertoire of commands neither has to be memorized nor constantly checked on a summary sheet; everything the user needs to know is always on the screen.

There are, however, different modes of operation for the program with which the user must become familiar. In the write/edit mode text is entered into the memory of the computer, and the cursor can be moved around in the text to allow corrections, additions, or deletions to be made. As with all word processors, the cursor position is the only place that changes or additions can be made to the text. In the print mode a copy of the text can be printed, or text can be saved onto or retrieved from a disk. First-time users sometimes have difficulty in becoming comfortable with the differences between these modes. All word processors have these functions, but many word processors allow users to shift among the functions without changing modes.

Several very useful options are built into this program. First, when the user wants to delete or move text, the program prompts with the question, "Do you really want to do this?" Even after the action is done, the user has one chance to undo the deletion or the move. Once any other action has been taken on the text, however, that chance is lost. In the print mode the program prompts the user with a list of questions that allow the line length, the page length, the spacing, pagination, and a variety of other format concerns to be set. When the printout is completed, the program asks if another copy is desired.

After some experimentation with the package, it becomes clear that there are real limits on the size of a document that can be written easily. Each text file that is created holds only about ten pages of material (about 2,300 words), so a very lengthy document would have to be written in pieces. Since files can be linked for printing, this is possible, but it does cause some awkwardness in writing anything lengthy.

Anderson (1983) in a review of this word processor stated that "I cannot think of any features I would demand of a $70 word processor that are missing from this package" (p. 34). While this may be an overstatement, it should be pointed out that some word-processing features are missing, though at the current cost of the package it might be unreasonable to expect them. For example, there is no way to produce form letters with individual names and addresses in the heading; and there is no capability to embed commands, so formatting a poem or an outline is quite awkward. Figures 9.1 and 9.2 show two of the screens that a student might encounter in using Bank Street Writer.

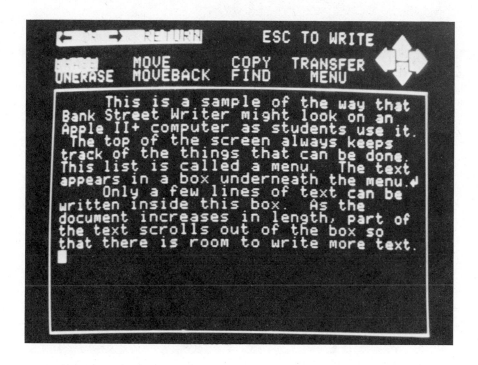

Figure 9.1 Edit mode

All in all, Bank Street Writer is quite a good word processor for simple documents. It would serve many useful purposes, both for students and for adults. During part of 1982–83, for example, Bank Street Writer was one of the top five most-often-purchased software packages in the home computer market. It is a package that can be shared by both adults and children, and that may be part of its appeal.

Some other word processors currently available for microcomputers include the following: (Of course, not all are appropriate for elementary school students.)

Apple Writer	Newscript
Atari Word Processor	Papermate
Easy Writer	Screenwriter II
Electric Pencil	Scripsit III
Lazy Writer	Super Text II

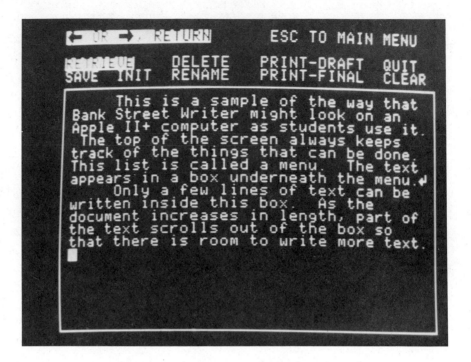

Figure 9.2   Write mode

Letter Perfect   Text Wizard
Letter Writer   Wordpro 4 Plus
Magic Wand   Wordstar
Magic Window   Write One
Mini Word Processor

New programs are frequently being introduced to the software market, so the buyer should try out several packages and read reviews that are available before spending the money necessary to get a good word processor. The packages listed above range in price from about twenty to about five hundred dollars, and some of them require additional hardware in order to operate properly. All of these considerations need to be taken into account prior to purchase. Also, not every package works on every microcomputer. In fact, most are specifically written for one or two kinds of hardware. This is obviously one of the major considerations that a buyer must consider. As with any purchase, you frequently get what you are willing to pay for. The more expensive the package, the more the user can and should demand from it.

WRITING EXERCISES TO USE
WITH A WORD PROCESSOR

Many different writing activities can be done with a word processor. They range from low-level drill and practice activities to sophisticated creative-writing activities, with many activities of intermediate difficulty in between. Many professional journals are devoting whole issues to word processing; for example, *The Computing Teacher* in May 1984. These special issues usually contain suggestions for ways to use word processors in classrooms.

A few activities are briefly described below, generally moving from less difficult to more difficult. The examples are provided partly as a starting point; teachers should expand them or combine them in whatever ways are most useful for a particular classroom setting.

1. *Sentence Combining.*   One of the lowest-level activities is sentence combining. A set of sentence pairs can be stored on a disk by the teacher. Students then retrieve that file from the disk and write a compound sentence to replace each pair of sentences in the file. The finished work can either be stored on a disk or printed out to hand in.

2. *Change Words.*   There are several forms of this activity, some more difficult that others. The simplest is for the teacher to prepare a short document (e.g., a paragraph) and store it on a disk. The students retrieve the document and change the tense of each of the verbs, or change the subjects and verbs from singular to plural. A more challenging activity is to "inflate" or "deflate" the number sounds in each word. For example, in the word *into* the "-to" sounds like *two*. To inflate this word the students would write "inthree," while to deflate this word they would write "inone." This type of activity creates conceptual nonsense, but it forces the students to analyze each

sound in each word, and it may be useful practice for skills like syllabication.

3. *Finish/Start a Story.*   The teacher could store the beginning (or the end) of a story on disk, and the students could finish (or start) that story. This activity gives practice at organizing sequences of events and allows for considerable creativity without forcing the students to begin with a blank page.

4. *Stream of Consciousness.*   One nice feature of word processing programs on computers is that if the monitor is turned off, but the computer is left on, information can still be typed into memory; the information is simply not visible on the screen. When the monitor is turned back on, the information will appear on the screen (as if by magic!). Turning the monitor off prevents a writer from looking back at what has been written; and if s/he has a strong urge to edit during that composing process, that urge has to be suppressed. This is a good technique for encouraging writers simply to write down their thoughts as a stream of consciousness. Then after the thoughts are written, they can be rearranged and edited as required.

5. *Electronic Newspaper.*   Students can create an electronic newspaper or magazine using a word processor. Individuals or teams can compose articles, and a review panel of students (i.e., the editorial board) can select the articles that are to be included in the "newspaper." Copies could be printed, or the newspaper could be kept solely in electronic form on disk. Students could then access the articles via the computer.

6. *Electronic Letter Writing.*   If modems and telephones are available, students in different rooms in the same school (or in different schools in town or even in different schools around the country) can write letters to each other on a word processor and then send them electronically. Several projects have been set up to allow students from different cultures to learn about each other in this way. Students get practice in writing and they have the motivation of talking with another student.

In the primary grades the first four of these activities would seem to be most appropriate. The content should be kept simple, but even very young children should be exposed to this means of writing. There is also a word-processing program, Write One (Purdy and Purdy, 1983) that has been developed especially for first-grade students. This program uses graphics to create large print on the screen and then prints the same characters when a printout is made.

In the intermediate grades all six of the activities are appropriate, though the last two would take special planning and equipment. As will be noted later, one of the consistent findings of word-processing research is that students tend to write more with a word processor. Creative writing is thus more likely to become a regular part of the language arts curriculum when a word processor is used. Students are more willing to write and they will likely write more. The focus of attention can really be on expression, with the mechanics taken care of during the editing phases of the activities.

RESEARCH ON THE USE OF WORD PROCESSORS

There appears to be relatively little research on the use of word processors to teach writing skills. As a consequence, the effects claimed for such use is often based on anecdotal information that may or may not truly represent stable effects that would be common across many teachers.

Henney (1983) studied the effects of type style on the monitor screen (all capitals or mixed upper and lower case) on the speed and comprehension of reading information. She used two samples, sixth-graders and prospective elementary school teachers. For the sixth-graders there appeared to be no difference either in speed or in comprehension of material for the two type styles. However, the students said they preferred the mixed style since it was more familiar. For the prospective teachers the mixed style was read faster, but the all-capitals style was read more accurately. (Perhaps the slower reading speed encouraged more attention to individual words and thus more attention to the meanings of those words.) Studies like this are very important, since the use of monitor displays is so new. The fact that the monitor is vertical instead of horizontal, as a printed page usually is, may also make an important difference in the way that students process the information they read. Until more research is carried out, teachers should not assume that the information on the monitor is being perceived in the same way as in a printed document.

In terms of the effects of word processors, rather than just the effects of computer displays, Daiute (1982) pointed out several effects in a brief, research survey article. First, writers who use computers tend to be less concerned about the errors they make, possibly because they know that errors are easy to correct. Too, the "prettiness" of the printed output of the word processor tends to give a "halo" effect to the judgment of the quality of the work. That is, writers may tend to see their work as better than it is, just because it looks good. Also, students who have serious motor-skill difficulties seem to be helped greatly by using a word processor; they are much better able to express their thoughts.

Second, computer writers tend to write longer works. There is no guarantee that the extra length adds anything to the quality.

Third, computer writers tend to revise more and to experiment more with rearrangements of words.

On the negative side of things, anyone who wants to use a word processor must learn the language of that system. That is, each program has special words or keys that instruct the word processor what to do. Depending on what the writing tasks are, learning to use these special commands may take many hours. But until those commands are basically mastered, the word processor may actually slow down the process of writing. The special words may constitute a minicomputer language, and learning this computer language may be somewhat difficult.

With the advent of more sophisticated computer technology, such as voice-driven computers, the use of word processors may become noticeably easier and more common. The initial difficulty in learning the special commands, for example, may be avoidable. Too, more electronic connections among computer terminals around the world may result in more written communication than is currently being used, but that communication may be via electronic transfer rather than in paper form.

Piper (1984) used word processing to teach sentence combining to fifth-graders. Her hope was to improve the syntactic maturity and the reading comprehension of the students. She used a case study approach; the experimental and control groups each contained two students above grade level on standardized test scores and two students below grade level. The treatment was forty-five minutes of sentence combining (via a word processor or in the traditional way) per day, twice a week, for eight weeks. On a posttest of writing the number of words per sentence and the number of embellishments (e.g., descriptive phrases) per sentence were greater for the experimental group than for the control group. However, there was no difference in reading comprehension between the two groups. This suggests that the objectives for word-processing activities should be fairly specific. Wide transfer should not be expected.

Riel (1985) helped third- and fourth-graders with learning difficulties in five schools in Alaska and California develop an electronic newspaper network over a twelve-week period. The students in the five schools traded stories (via disks sent through the mail), and an editorial board in each school selected the stories that it wanted for its own newspaper. All of the stories were written by student teams so that there was peer interaction, team editing, and peer review during the composing stage of each story.

Although no striking change in the cognitive skills of the students occurred, their attitudes toward writing did appear to be significantly improved. They were eager to write and to share their writing with other people, such as parents. The stories they wrote also changed during the course of the project. The number of words increased, and the focus of the stories changed from talking about things (static) to talking about activities (active). In describing activities, students by the end of the project were better able to sequence events clearly and correctly. There were also changes in the criteria used to select the stories for inclusion in the newspaper, but these differences seem to be less quantifiable.

Sharples (1983) described an experimental writing package, adaptable for home computers, that was designed to assist children in developing their writing skills. Many of the features of this package are similar to features of word processors, but there were unusual features as well. Students could create "nonsense" sentences or short stories by having the computer pick words of a particular type (e.g., noun) from lists of words of that type entered earlier by the student. Text could also be transformed by substitution of words, by combining sentences or phrases, or by using a self-contained thesaurus to find nearly-equivalent words. The package seemed effective for a trial group of six eleven-year-olds, though more experimentation is called for to verify its effectiveness. The creativity of the package suggests that home computers can soon be expected to have the capability both to teach writing skills and to let writers take advantage of word-processing capabilities.

Lewis and Mack (1982) examined the difficulties that adults had in learning by themselves a text-processing system. Although the subjects were adults, the difficulties identified may apply to elementary school students whenever they are expected to learn even vaguely similar content on their own. First, learners have trouble following directions, and they try to learn-by-doing without appreciating how preparation (e.g., reading the directions) might help. Second, learners have trouble coordinating directions with the actions involving the keyboard. This may represent cognitive overload, too much information to deal with. Third, failure with one step in a sequence may make the remaining steps impossible to follow because they do not match what is happening on the screen. The net result of these difficulties is that learners lose track of their goals, and the learning experience reduces to more-or-less random trials.

In addition, learners tend to fill in their understanding with intuitions or inferences about the material to be learned. These intuitions are often wrong; and as a result, learners' generalizations are often equally wrong. Compounding this phenomenon are difficulties in determining what information is relevant. Frequently all information is treated as equally relevant, in spite of the fact that this is only seldom true.

Teachers must obviously be alert for signs of these difficulties, even when instruction is carefully sequenced. It is sometimes hard for experienced people (e.g., teachers) to empathize with the difficulties of naive people (e.g., students).

CONCLUSION

The research on the use of word processors is in its infancy. Of course, until the technology of word processing became available, its use was only a dream. Word processors have not been available long enough for many studies to be conceptualized and executed. Researchers are just beginning to identify appropriate questions to ask about the effects of word processors. By the end of the decade much more should be known about the effects in teaching writing and language arts. Undoubtedly there will be some positive effects, and some new instructional approaches can be carried out that previously were impossible. But teachers should not expect word processors to be a "cure-all" for problems in teaching language arts. Indeed, teachers will be faced with a critical question of what language arts skills and concepts are most important in a world that takes word processing for granted. That is a difficult question to answer, but it is probably the most important question to ask.

Computer Literacy

10

Computer literacy has become one of the "buzz words" of the 1980s. This seems to have happened primarily because the dramatic advances in computer technology have had an enormous impact on all aspects of life, especially on education. All educators are faced with the challenge of dealing with computers in many ways that could not even have been imagined as few as five years earlier.

At this point each person's approach to computer literacy must be to a great extent personal. Computer literacy is an area for which there are not yet many consensus positions. Until some stability is attained in defining this concept, heated debates, more emotional than rational, will likely continue over both definitions and the range of application of those definitions. There has also been speculation that the whole debate will become mute as the current generation of elementary school children reaches adulthood and carries with them skill at using computer technology. Perhaps so, but for today, computer literacy is a necessary concern of teachers.

WHAT IS COMPUTER LITERACY FOR THE 1980s?

A definition of computer literacy must be built on an implicit assumption of what literacy means in general. One approach to literacy is that it signifies the minimum needed to get by in that area. A second approach is that it means that one is truly educated about that area. There are frequent shifts between these two definitions; for example, on the one hand there is concern about the percentage of the population that is functionally literate (the minimum approach), and on the other hand specific people are praised for being so literate (the fully educated approach). The kind of definition accepted for computer literacy depends greatly on the underlying assumption that is made about the particular kind of literacy.

From the view of the minimum approach, computer literacy probably would mean that a person knows enough about computers to get by in the world. It would be expected that such a person would know some terminology (e.g., hardware, software, input, output), some facts about the ways that computers are used in the world, and minimal information about the kinds of software that are available (e.g., word processing, games, educational software).

From the view of the fully educated approach, much more would be expected. A fully educated, computer-literate person might be expected to know how to program in one of the standard computer languages (e.g., LOGO, BASIC, Pascal) and to be able to use the computer to solve some simple problems (that is, to be able to use the computer as a tool). In addition, that person might have much more sophisticated familiarity with terminology and with the impact of computers on society, both in today's world and in the world of the future.

In one sense the difference between these two definitions is exemplified by the positions on computer literacy taken by Anderson and Klassen (1981) and Luehrmann (1981). Anderson and Klassen conducted an extensive study of the kinds of things that teachers were teaching about computers. They then used this information to formulate a definition of computer literacy that in a real sense represented the position of most computer-teaching teachers in the late 1970s and early 1980s. Their objectives for computer literacy spanned ideas such as the following:

1. applications: current uses of computers and general considerations for applying computers to new situations

2. hardware: terminology of a computer system
3. impact: positive and negative effects of computerization in society
4. limitations: capabilities and limitations of computers as machines
5. programming/algorithms: read, modify, interpret, and construct computer programs and algorithms
6. software and data processing: terminology of software in general, and information processing systems in particular
7. usage: motor and procedural skills for operating a computer or a computer terminal
8. values and feelings: attitudes toward personal use of computer and toward computers as a social force

Although their article goes into some depth on specifying sub-objectives for each of these areas, Anderson and Klassen state that the amount that anyone ought to know about each depends on many factors. It would, for example, be possible for a person only to exhibit literacy on a multiple-choice test of regurgitated information and yet to meet the computer-literacy objectives of Anderson and Klassen. Thus, in one sense, this is a minimalist's view of computer literacy.

Luehrmann on the other hand takes the position that people are not computer-literate until they can talk in a computer language; that is, not until they can program. He assumes that most of the other kinds of objectives that Anderson and Klassen list will develop more or less automatically once one begins to interact with a computer. Expecting this much generalization and transfer is probably unreasonable. Yet in at least some of the areas (e.g., feelings about personal computing) most likely hands-on experience is essential.

In terms of the current capabilities of computers there is probably a strong argument for requiring that a computer-literate person be able to program. For many tasks that one might want computers to do there is no available software to accomplish the task. In this case, there may be little choice but to write an appropriate program or to forego that particular task. However, in terms of the possible future development of both hardware and software, computer technology may become so user-friendly that it may become unnecessary for most people to know how to program, at least in the sense of learning a special language for writing programs. In the not-too-distant future it may be possible literally to talk to computers and to get them to perform without having to sit down and write programs, or even having to obtain special software. Many functions may be built into the hardware, and that hardware may be able to recognize spoken English.

These two positions on computer literacy contrast the notions of minimal and fully educated literacy, simply applied to the area of computers. The particular position that anyone takes will probably reflect her/his general position on what literacy means. Teachers must identify the underlying assumptions of any participant in a discussion of computer literacy.

Deringer and Molnar (1982), in summarizing a national conference of computer literacy, noted that computer literacy for the 1980s is necessary, both collectively for the survival of the U.S. and individually for participation in the emerging "knowledge" society (p. 4). They also identified several key components for achieving computer literacy.

1. recognition that computer literacy is multifaceted
2. identification and development of knowledgeable people both to create new tools and materials and to effectively use those that are available
3. involvement of home, workplace, and community in developing computer literacy
4. presence of computers for instruction in all schools and for all students
5. availability of high-quality curricula and courseware
6. continued innovation, research, and development to identify new opportunities for using computers (pp. 5–7)

While these concepts are certainly general and might apply to many kinds of literacy, too often it seems that presentations about computer literacy ignore most of them, to the detriment of a thorough understanding of the range of notions encompassed by the term *computer literacy*.

WHAT IS COMPUTER LITERACY FOR 1990 AND BEYOND?

In order to determine what computer literacy might be for the next generation of students, it is necessary to try to identify the underlying computer-literacy concepts. That is, what is it about computer literacy that is not likely to change and is definitely not dependent on the particular hardware and software available at the moment? Those general concepts will form the core of a useful understanding of computer literacy for the 1990s.

One fundamental aspect of computer literacy is that the literate person knows how to discuss computer-related ideas. That is, basic terminology is important and is likely to remain so. The underlying terminology seems to include terms related to the conceptual organization of the hardware (e.g., memory, central processor, external storage), to the interactions of people with the machines (e.g., input, output, hardware, software, terminal, modem), and to the special informational structures that a computer environment demands (e.g., data base, disk storage). A computer-literate person must be able to deal with these concepts.

A second fundamental part of computer literacy is understanding the changing ways that computers impact on our lives. For example, currently there is a lot of talk about the use of robots to replace traditional blue-collar workers. A computer-literate person needs to know that these robots are in fact run by computers and that the miniaturization of computer technology will soon mean the increased use of robots in much more than menial jobs. The notion of what computer-driven technology is capable of doing is undoubtedly going to expand greatly, and computer-literate people need to have a context within which to understand this expanding concept.

In particular, the development of easily accessible and easily searched data bases will turn many "professional" tasks into computer-operated activities. One of the most frequently encountered may be visits to the doctor. Computers can already be programmed to take medical histories and to make preliminary diagnoses based on the symptoms given by the patient. (In fact, in some areas of medicine, like alcoholism, computer diagnosis is already demonstrating itself to be more accurate than human diagnosis, partly because patients are more willing to give accurate information to the computer than to a human interviewer.) In the near future, computer diagnosis of ordinary illnesses may be common and may even be conducted by telephone or by interactive computer hookups over telephone lines. Physicians may in turn be able to spend more time with patients, particularly at the point in an examination at which critical information needs to be gathered and at which the patient needs the most individual attention. The computer will have done the tedious, initial data-gathering activities. Thus, the increased use of computer technology may actually increase the personal interaction of professionals with their clients, while at the same time allowing more efficient use of the professionals' time.

A third aspect of computer literacy that is likely not to change over the years is knowledge of the tasks for which software is available, or for which specialized computers are being manufactured. A computer-literate person needs to know that a computer can act as an efficient word processor, a speedy budget planner, a tireless record keeper, a clever player of games, and a patient tutor for educational purposes; and for each of these tasks a wide variety of software is available. With this knowledge, the computer-literate person can take advantage of the power of computers. Without this knowledge, s/he probably would continue to perform these tasks in ways that are traditional for her or him. There would be no improvement in the quality of life because of lack of knowledge that improvement was possible.

At the same time, one needs to be careful not to limit the perception of what computers can do to the level of current computer software. Creative people will continue to design new solutions to old problems (and indeed new solutions to new problems), and a computer-literate person needs to attempt to stay more or less current on those new solutions.

Finally, a fundamental concept of computer literacy is knowledge of the special languages of computers. Given the current state of technology, this probably means that a computer-literate person needs to know how to program at a simple level. From one perspective some computer applications like word processing might be conceptualized as a specialized computer language. All of the currently available word processors require the user to learn a set of specialized commands in order to make the package operate. These commands are sequenced in different orders to accomplish different tasks, though these commands are usually used only in immediate execution mode; there is no option to write a word processing "program." Thus, learning to use a word processor might be roughly equivalent to learning to program.

Too, it is quite believable that in the future the language of the computer will be ordinary spoken English, though probably with a very limited vocabulary. When this happens, proper use of English may become critical in order to make use of computer technology. There will be no special language required for many applications.

COMPUTER LITERACY FOR
THE ELEMENTARY SCHOOL

Hunter (1982) in discussing aspects of computer literacy for the elementary school gives perspectives of both the current state of affairs and the potential for the future. In both cases her focus seems to be on the underlying concepts that support computer literacy. In terms of the current state of affairs, she identifies four main areas: (a) using computer programs, (b) procedural thinking, (c) computer applications, and (d) social and values implications of computer/communications systems (p. 219). In the area of applications, for example, she suggests that it is important for students to learn to think in terms of the general systems that might be encountered. Thus, notions of user, uses, output, input, and data base are the critical concerns. Understanding these notions will give students flexibility, but only if they gain firsthand experience with different uses of computers. Merely being aware that there are different uses of computers is not sufficient.

The resulting flexibility will allow students to adapt to whatever situation they are in, instead of being bound by the particular, perhaps rotely learned, information that was presented in class. Particular applications are to be viewed as instances of the general concepts and help to enhance students' understanding of those general concepts.

In the long term, Hunter optimistically projects that students will have in the schools much of the same computer technology that is being used in the real world. Further, all students will develop the skills needed to take advantage of that technology. Students will address more sophisticated problems than are currently being addressed in school curricula and will have the resources, both physical and intellectual, to solve them. Communication will be the overriding focus of activity, and a culture of social responsibility about how to use information will be built into the curriculum.

If this vision is even close to being correct, there will need to be pervasive changes in the ways that education is provided to students. But without a start now on the development of computer literacy in the elementary school, there is no hope that such a vision could be correct. Teachers must themselves first acquire the knowledge with which to approach the task of preparing students for full participation in the information society of the next century. Otherwise, teachers may find themselves to be so uninformed that they can no longer effectively communicate with students.

COMPUTER LITERACY IN THE PRIMARY GRADES

Computer literacy in the primary grades has implicitly been defined in the preceding chapters. That is, primary-grade students should be exposed to some CAI (e.g., drill and practice or tutorial), some tool uses of computers (e.g., word processing), and some programming and problem solving on the computer. All of these pieces fit into the general concept of computer literacy, and in fact the notion of computer literacy seems merely to pull the pieces together into one whole. Bitter (1982), for example, has provided a scope and sequence chart of some computer-literacy components, much of which is consistent with the general definition outlined in this chapter. The Cupertino, California, School District (Cupertino, 1983) has also provided a scope and sequence chart for computer-literacy objectives for elementary school. For the time being, separate computer-literacy units designed to teach concepts like those in these charts are likely to be the best way to proceed. These units will gradually be replaced with integration of computer literacy into other activities.

COMPUTER LITERACY IN THE INTERMEDIATE GRADES

There is more need to implement specific computer-literacy units in the intermediate grades, for these students will soon face the need to use computers in junior and senior high schools. One attempt to organize computer-literacy units at this level has been made by Alberta Education, the provincial department of education in Alberta, Canada. Their scope and sequence chart is presented in Figure 10.1.

It is probably significant that the only objective that crosses all three grades is Topic 2: How to use a computer. Using prepared programs (including tool programs), showing responsibility in using the equipment, and feeling confident about one's ability to control the computer are very important characteristics of a computer-literate person, regardless of the particular definition of computer literacy. It is also important that no particular computer language is specified in Topic 3, though LOGO is mentioned in the notes. More has already been said about the choice of language in Chapter 8.

Another sequence has been prepared by the U.S. Department of Defense Dependents Schools (1982). Quite a bit of overlap exists between the two lists, but programming is referred to as computer science rather than computer literacy in the U.S. list (Figures 10.2 and 10.3).

HOW IMPORTANT IS COMPUTER LITERACY?

It should be obvious that computer literacy is already a very important part of the background of any elementary school teacher, and it will

CORE COMPONENTS

Topic 1: How computers do their work

Goals: 1. To develop student understanding of basic computer
                operations and terminology.
            2. To develop an appreciation of the technological
                development of computer systems.

OBJECTIVES	DIMENSION STATUS	GRADE 4	5	6	SUBJECT CORRELATION SOCIAL STUDIES/LANGUAGE ARTS/MATHEMATICS
The student will:					
1.0 DESCRIBE THE BASIC OPERATIONS AND HISTORY OF COMPUTER SYSTEMS					
1.1 Identify the major parts of a computer.	A	X			1.1 - 1.3 Language Arts - Grades 4, 5, 6 - Read increasingly complex material with fluency; speak/write fluently about increasingly complex subjects.
1.2 Describe in his/ her words the terms "hardware" and "software" and list examples of each.	A	X			Demonstrate continuing growth in oral/written vocabulary (breadth and depth) by using: increasingly precise vocabulary.
1.3 Describe in his/ her words what is meant by "input" and "output" and give examples of each.	A	X			
1.4 Recognize that a computer gets instructions from a program written by a person.	A	X			1.4 Language Arts - Grades 4, 5, 6 - Identify and infer relationships, e.g. time, cause and effect.

NOTE: Dimension Codes   -- A = Awareness; F = Function;
                             U = Critical Understanding.
       Hands-On Required -- *
       Recommended grade if unit is taught across Division II grades -- X

Figure 10.1 Alberta Education Computer Literacy Scope and Sequence for Elementary School

OBJECTIVES	DIMENSION STATUS	GRADE			SUBJECT CORRELATION SOCIAL STUDIES/LANGUAGE ARTS/MATHEMATICS
		4	5	6	
1.5 Identify the similarities and differences among computers, calculators and electronic games.	A		X		1.5 Math – Use a calculator and a computer as a computational tool in problem-solving situations (Appendix IV, Elementary Mathematics Curriculum Guide, 1982). – Use a calculator and a computer in Extension and Enrichment activities (10% allocation of Math time).
1.6 Recognize that computers are best suited to tasks requiring speed, accuracy, repeated operations and processing of large amounts data.	A	X			
1.7 Recognize the rapid changes in computer capabilities since the 1940's.	A	X			1.7 Social Studies – Topic 4B – Inquiry Questions 7 and 8: 7. What are some ways in which lifestyles today differ from lifestyles during the settlement era, the Great Depression and World War II? Are there differences in such areas as employment, leisure time activities, education and availability of material goods? 8. What might life be like when today's grade four students are adults? Might there be new and different kinds of occupations, leisure time activities and ways to learn new skills?
1.8 Explain the basic operation of a computer in terms of input, processing and output of data.	A	X			1.8 Language Arts – Grades 4, 5, 6 – Speak/write fluently about increasingly complex subjects.
1.9 Recognize the relationship of input to the result or output.	A	X			1.9 Math – Step 4 in the Problem-Solving process (assess the process on the basis of the answer or resulting product).
1.10 Recognize that people control what computers do.	A	X			1.10 Language Arts – Grades 4, 5, 6 – Identify and infer relationships e.g. cause and effect.
	Hours	5	1	0	

Figure 10.1   *(continued)*

Topic 2:   How to use a computer

Goal: To develop student skills, attitudes and interests which
           facilitate the use of computer systems.

OBJECTIVES	DIMENSION STATUS	GRADE 4	GRADE 5	GRADE 6	SUBJECT CORRELATION SOCIAL STUDIES/LANGUAGE ARTS/MATHEMATICS
The student will:					
2.0 USE A COMPUTER SYSTEM					Computer Literacy objectives 2.1-2.4, inclusive.
2.1 Use a prepared program in a computer.	F*	X	X	X	All Subjects – Use available evaluated course-ware to achieve objectives specified for selected subject areas (see Section III – Software).
2.2 Show respect and responsibility for equipment and other users' materials (e.g. follow safety and scheduling rules).	AF*	X	X	X	Social Studies – Grades 4, 5, 6 – Use a word processor to develop some of the communication skills specified under "Participation Skills". Language Arts – Grades 4, 5, 6 – Use a word processor to write -- well-organized paragraphs, apply proofreading skills with increasing competence, prepare a simple bibliography acknowledging author, title --- of book.
2.3 Use system commands to load and run programs.	F*	X	X	X	2.2 Social Studies – Grades 4, 5, 6 – Develop some of the group decision-making skills specified under "Participation Skills" when establishing scheduling and safety rules for computer use.
2.4 Feel confident about his/her ability to use and control computers.	AF*	X	X	X	
	Hours	2	3	1	

Figure 10.1   *(continued)*

Topic 3:   How to make computers work for you

Goal: To have students appreciate that effective problem-solving
           with computer systems requires the application of logical
           thought processes and develop the skills required for a
           holistic, systematic approach to problem-solving.

OBJECTIVES	DIMENSION STATUS	GRADE 4	5	6	SUBJECT CORRELATION SOCIAL STUDIES/LANGUAGE ARTS/MATHEMATICS
The student will:					
3.0 FOLLOW AN ORDERLY SEQUENCE OF STEPS TO DEVELOP A COMPUTER PROGRAM TO SOLVE A PARTICULAR PROBLEM					
3.1 Recognize that a computer program is an ordered series of instructions that allows a computer to perform tasks.	A		X		3.1 - 3.5 Math - Grades 4, 5, 6 - Apply problem-solving strategies to create a simple computer program that solves a word problem specified in one of the Prescribed Resources. OR Use the LOGO language to facilitate problem-solving to attain the specified Geometry objectives.
3.2 Order specific steps in a procedure to accomplish a task.	F		X		OR Use the LOGO language for Enrichment and Extension Topic: Networks. 3.2 and 3.3 Language Arts - Grades 4, 5, 6 - Demonstrate growth in thought processes by perceiving and comprehending increasingly complex spoken and/
3.3 Find and correct errors in a procedure to perform a task.	F		X		or illustrated: sequence. Demonstrate growth in thought processes by perceiving and comprehending increasingly complex written and/or illustrated: sequence. Demonstrate growth in thought processes by expressing orally increasingly complex: sequence.
3.4 Create and save a simple computer program.	F*		X		Demonstrate growth in thought processes by expressing in writing increasingly complex: sequence.
3.5 Check computer output to ensure results are reasonable.	F*		X		3.5 Language Arts - Grades 4, 5, 6 - Read/view increasingly complex material critically to evaluate or judge ideas.
	Hours	0	6	0	

Figure 10.1   *(continued)*

Topic 4:   How computers are used and what they can and cannot do

Goal: To have students appraise the applications, limitations and capabilities of computer.

OBJECTIVES	DIMENSION STATUS	GRADE 4	GRADE 5	GRADE 6	SUBJECT CORRELATION SOCIAL STUDIES/LANGUAGE ARTS/MATHEMATICS
The student will:					
4.0 DESCRIBE THE BASIC APPLICA-TIONS, LIMITA-TIONS, AND CAPABILITIES OF COMPUTERS.					
4.1 Identify the areas in society where computers are used (e.g. banking, manufacturing, transportation, medicine, recreation, the home, the library, publishing, creative arts, education).	A	X			4.1 and 4.2 Social Studies - Topic 4A - Inquiry Question 6: 6. How has technology assisted in the location, development and use of natural resources in Alberta? - Topic 4B - Inquiry Question 7: 7. What are some ways in which lifestyles today differ from lifestyles during the settlement era, the Great Depression and World War II? Are there differences in such areas as employment, leisure time activities, education, and availability of material goods?
4.2 Identify the tasks performed by computers in these areas.	A	X			- Topic 4C - Inquiry Question 4: 4. What transportation and communication links are used to connect Alberta to the rest of Canada and the world?
4.3 Recognize that computers cannot "think" in the way we normally use the word "think".	U			X	Language Arts - Grades 4, 5, 6 - Demonstrate growth in thought processes by perceiving and comprehending increasingly complex written and/or illustrated: descriptions, explanations, summaries, comparisons. Read a widening variety of material suitable to grade (four, five, six) in the following forms: report, interview.
4.4 Recognize that there are a number of things computers cannot do such as make value judgements and provide answers to every question.	U			X	Note: Comparable Language Arts objectives are also specified for Listening/Viewing, Speaking and Writing skills.
4.5 Describe the similarities and differences between computers in fiction and real computers.	U			X	4.3, 4.4 and 4.5 Language Arts - Grades 4, 5, 6 Read increasingly complex material critically to evaluate or judge ideas: discriminating fact from opinion, fiction from non-fiction, relevance from irrelevance.
Hours		3	0	3	

Figure 10.1   *(continued)*

> Topic 5:   How computers affect society
>
> Goal: To have students assess the current and potential impact
>   of computers on society.

OBJECTIVES	DIMENSION STATUS	GRADE 4	5	6	SUBJECT CORRELATION SOCIAL STUDIES/LANGUAGE ARTS/MATHEMATICS
The student will:					
5.0 APPRECIATE THE IMPACT COMPUTERS CAN HAVE ON OUR LIFESTYLE.					5.1 and 5.3 Social Studies - Topic 4A - Inquiry Question 6: 6. How has technology assisted in the location, development and use of natural resources in Alberta?
5.1 Describe how a computer can affect him/ herself as he/ she assumes various roles, e.g. student, consumer, worker, citizen.	U			X	- Topic 4B - Inquiry Questions 7 and 8: Participation Skills 1 and 2 7. What are some ways in which lifestyles today differ from lifestyles during the settlement era, the Great Depression and World War II. Are there differences in such areas as employment, leisure time activities, education and availability of material goods? 8. What might life be like when today's grade four students are adults? Might there be
5.2 Recognize that alleged "computer mistakes" are usually mistakes made by people.	U			X	new and different kinds of occupations, leisure time activities and ways to learn new skills? 1. Communicate effectively by orally expressing opinions about the use of work and leisure time. 2. Interpret ideas and feelings of others by
5.3 Recognize that computers are machines designed and operated by humans to assist in many tasks.	U			X	demonstrating an understanding of different decisions made about adjustment to change at the personal level. - Topic 4C - Inquiry Questions 4 and 7: 4. What transportation and communication links are used to connect Alberta to the rest of the world? (Consider air, rail, media networks, telecommunications, etc.) 7. How are Albertans affected by the "shrinking" nature of the modern world? - Topic 5B - Inquiry Question 6: 6. What forms of employment are associated with resource development? - Topic 5C - Inquiry Question 4: 4. What are some of the important linkages that exist today between Canada and the United States? (Consider economic, political, and cultural affairs.)
	Hours	0	0	6	

Figure 10.1   *(continued)*

OBJECTIVES	DIMENSION STATUS	GRADE 4 5 6	SUBJECT CORRELATION SOCIAL STUDIES/LANGUAGE ARTS/MATHEMATICS
			– Topic 6B – Inquiry Questions 5 and 6: 5. What problems do Eastern societies face for which Western technology might provide partial solutions? 6. What problems do Western societies face for which Eastern societies might provide partial solutions? 5.1, 5.2 and 5.3 Language Arts – Grades 4, 5, 6 – Speak/write fluently about increasingly complex subjects.

Figure 10.1   *(continued)*

become increasingly important in the 1990s and beyond. It is at least equally important for elementary school students.

Pressures from school boards and parents to integrate microcomputers into the elementary school curriculum make it critical that teachers have knowledge of the uses of that technology. Teachers cannot ignore computer technology as they may have done with innovations like educational television or programmed instruction, precisely because the drive for use of computers is coming from the home (and thus the tax base) rather than just from other professionals. In most previous instances of educational innovation, teachers found themselves having to justify to the school board why money should be spent on acquiring that innovation. In the case of microcomputers, teachers find themselves in the position of having to answer the question of why the innovation is *not* being used. It is not uncommon for teachers to find unrequested microcomputers delivered to the classroom door with the full expectation that teachers will make the best use of them. Obviously this cannot be done unless teachers have the knowledge available to accomplish this task.

For the foreseeable future, it is quite possible that at least some of the students in every elementary school will be more knowledgeable

1.0 | Computer Literacy

THE STUDENT WILL BE ABLE TO ...	Demonstrate Understanding of the Capabilities, Applications, and Implications of Computer Technology

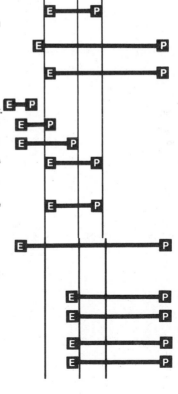

PROGRAM OBJECTIVES:	INSTRUCTIONAL OBJECTIVES:
1.1 Interact with a computer and/or other electronic devices.	**1.1.1** Demonstrate ability to operate a variety of devices which are based on electronic logic.
	1.1.2 Demonstrate ability to use a computer in the interactive mode.
	1.1.3 Independently select a program from the computer resource library.
	1.1.4 Recognize user errors associated with computer utilization.
1.2 Explain the functions and uses of a computer system.	**1.2.1** Use an appropriate vocabulary for communicating about computers.
	1.2.2 Distinguish between interactive mode and batch mode computer processing.
	1.2.3 Identify a computer system's major components such as input, memory, processing, and output.
	1.2.4 Recognize tasks for which computer utilization is appropriate.
	1.2.5 Describe the major historical developments in computing.
1.3 Utilize systematic processes in problem solving.	**1.3.1** Choose a logical sequence of steps needed to perform a task.
	1.3.2 Diagram the steps in solving a problem.
	1.3.3 Select the appropriate tool and procedure to solve a problem.
	1.3.4 Develop systematic procedures to perform useful tasks in areas such as social studies, business, science, and mathematics.
	1.3.5 Write simple programs to solve problems using a high-level language such as PILOT, LOGO, and BASIC.
1.4 Appraise the impact of computer technology upon human life.	**1.4.1** Identify specific uses of computers in fields such as medicine, law enforcement, industry, business, transportation, government, banking, and space exploration.
	1.4.2 Compare computer-related occupations and careers.
	1.4.3 Identify social and other non-technical factors which might restrict computer utilization.
	1.4.4 Recognize the consequences of computer utilization.
	1.4.5 Differentiate between responsible and irresponsible uses of computer technology.

Figure 10.2 U.S. Department of Defense Schools' Computer Literacy Sequence

2.0 Computer Science

THE STUDENT WILL BE ABLE TO ...

Demonstrate Understandings of Computer Systems Including Software Development, the Design and Operation of Hardware, and the Use of Computer Systems in Solving Problems.

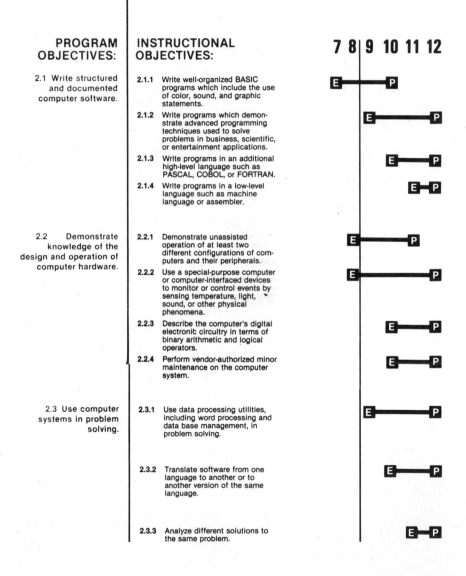

PROGRAM OBJECTIVES:	INSTRUCTIONAL OBJECTIVES:	7 8 9 10 11 12
2.1 Write structured and documented computer software.	**2.1.1** Write well-organized BASIC programs which include the use of color, sound, and graphic statements.	E———P
	2.1.2 Write programs which demonstrate advanced programming techniques used to solve problems in business, scientific, or entertainment applications.	E————P
	2.1.3 Write programs in an additional high-level language such as PASCAL, COBOL, or FORTRAN.	E——P
	2.1.4 Write programs in a low-level language such as machine language or assembler.	E-P
2.2 Demonstrate knowledge of the design and operation of computer hardware.	**2.2.1** Demonstrate unassisted operation of at least two different configurations of computers and their peripherals.	E———P
	2.2.2 Use a special-purpose computer or computer-interfaced devices to monitor or control events by sensing temperature, light, sound, or other physical phenomena.	E————P
	2.2.3 Describe the computer's digital electronic circuitry in terms of binary arithmetic and logical operators.	E——P
	2.2.4 Perform vendor-authorized minor maintenance on the computer system.	E——P
2.3 Use computer systems in problem solving.	**2.3.1** Use data processing utilities, including word processing and data base management, in problem solving.	E———P
	2.3.2 Translate software from one language to another or to another version of the same language.	E——P
	2.3.3 Analyze different solutions to the same problem.	E-P

Figure 10.3   U.S. Department of Defense Schools' Computer Science Sequence

about computers than any of the teachers in that school. This, too, is a departure from previous innovations. This is going to create a demand from the students that their teachers become computer-literate. The students are going to develop their own expertise because they have access to equipment at home, and the students' hunger for information is going to force teachers to gain equivalent information for themselves. Fortunately, it is possible to let students teach other students for a while, but ultimately teachers will need to gain enough expertise to forestall serious negative consequences of students' investigating sensitive areas (e.g., illegal copying, gaining access to presumably protected data bases) without adult supervision.

Too, in order to develop ethical computer behavior among students it will be necessary for adults to model such ethical behavior. This is not possible if adults are constantly relying on the students for all of the technical information. Students then would have to simultaneously generate their own system of ethical behavior. It is doubtful, especially at the elementary school level, that this will occur, at least in ways that are satisfactory to adults.

From the students' perspective, computer literacy is necessary if they are to become successful in the world into which they will graduate. Presumably, gaining adequate familiarity with computer technology will take time, and students will need to begin early to investigate computer tools (e.g., word processing), if they are to be comfortable with the full capabilities of those tools.

One of the dangers of current trends in computer use is that it seems to be becoming a male-dominated domain. In other areas, such as mathematics, the development of this perception occurs most intensely in about the junior high school years. If this is to be avoided in the future in the area of computer use (as indeed it *must* be), then familiarity with computer technology needs to be developed in elementary school years.

HOW DO TEACHERS DEVELOP THEIR OWN COMPUTER LITERACY?

Developing one's own computer literacy is, even under the best of circumstances, a time-consuming task. The options that are available, however, are like those open for any kind of professional development.

If possible, the best time to develop expertise is during the teacher preparation program prior to the point of entry into teaching. It is necessary, of course, to update the information acquired in this way at frequent intervals, but it is much easier to update information than to build knowledge from scratch.

Teachers already in the field do not have this convenient option. They must build computer literacy often from a base of no prior experience either with computers or with computer applications. These people have three choices: (a) take advantage of special in-service courses or workshops offered in their districts, (b) enroll in graduate courses at local colleges or universities, or (c) gather information on their own through talking with colleagues, reading, and attending professional meetings.

Many school districts are organizing special programs on computer literacy for their teachers. These range from an hour or two of conversation to several weeks of meetings with hands-on experience with microcomputers. Most of these are designed to provide only initial exposure to the concepts of computer literacy, and the prospects for follow-up, either through providing more detailed information or through actual use of computers in the classroom, are typically small. Thus, these programs are likely to whet the appetite but are not likely to provide the depth of knowledge that many teachers will ultimately need.

Colleges and universities in the U.S. and Canada are now beginning to develop special courses for teachers on the use of computers and microcomputers. Some of these courses are programming courses for teachers, while others are courses on the use of computer-assisted instructional materials or computer-managed instructional materials. The educational programming courses typically have fewer prerequisites than ordinary computer science courses and deal with the writing of programs that teachers might find useful in classroom situations; they may also be based on computer languages that are especially appropriate for school-age children. Because of the huge demand for technically oriented or business-oriented computer science classes, it is probably necessary right now for special classes to be set up for teachers. However, the disadvantage is that teachers do not get the cross-fertilization that comes from interaction with people with different perspectives. In the long term this may be a serious disadvantage because school-age students are going to want to know about those other uses of computers. Without some exposure to those applications, teachers might find themselves inadequately prepared to deal with the concerns of their students.

The last option of trying to gather sufficient information on one's own is not recommended for most teachers as the way to develop adequate knowledge of computer literacy. Computer technology is a technical field, and it is difficult to get very far in developing understanding without some guidance from someone who possesses at least some of that technical knowledge. Most teachers will find that gaining entry to this information will be considerably easier if they work with someone who is comfortable with the information. Once entry-level information is acquired, then reading professional literature and attending professional meetings are extremely productive ways to stay abreast of the field. Because computer technology is changing so rapidly, it is difficult to stay current. Most articles in journals, for example, are already out of date by the time they are published; the lag time needed for preparation of the manuscript is too great. Presentations at professional meetings are much more likely to contain the most recent information.

Too, as with most areas of in-service education, in talking to colleagues it is extremely comforting to find out that one's own difficulties in dealing with computer literacy (or the teaching of computer literacy) are not unique. Others' solutions to these difficulties can be discussed and then applied to one's own situation.

HOW DO TEACHERS HELP CHILDREN DEVELOP COMPUTER LITERACY?

One way to assist children in becoming computer-literate is to develop special curricula for use in a particular school. This is probably only a stopgap method of filling in the lack of information among students; students are not going to deal with computers in the real world as a separate entity. Rather, computers are going to be integrated into most of the activities that people engage in. Teachers, therefore, need to take a longer-range look at the needs of their students.

Bell (1982) has presented one accepted approach to taking this longer-term view. He argues strongly against the "buy it (i.e., computers), find a place to put it, figure out what to do with it, then find people to do it" approach that is all too common in dealing with microcomputers (p. 170). Instead, he outlines several steps for a more orderly and probably much more successful approach.

First, plan for the use of microcomputers and computer literacy. The planning group should contain people who have experience with computers and computer literacy (perhaps from outside the school district), people who are familiar with the functioning of the local district (e.g., teachers, administrators, and physical plant operators), and people who will have the responsibility to implement the program that is developed. Of importance to this planning are the opinions of parents on the ways that computers should be used and the opinions of students on what they would like to learn, or believe that they need to learn, about computers. The program will need the support of the local community in order to be successful, and attempts should be made to secure that cooperation before the program starts. Also be sure that plans are virtually complete before beginning. Don't try to implement a program piecemeal, with only some of the areas covered. Problems are much more likely to develop with this approach.

Second, gather information on the ways that computers can be used, and decide how they will be used in the local situation. This is probably the most important step, for it is this decision that will determine the structure of the local program. This decision will drive the choice of the equipment, the amount of equipment needed, and the nature and extent of the teacher in-service required.

Third, select the types of hardware to purchase. This choice will depend on many factors: (a) the ways in which the computers are to be used, (b) the current state of available equipment, (c) cost, (d) the amount of available resources, and (e) the number and kinds of peripherals needed. Of these, the most important consideration is probably the first. If there are going to be multiple uses of the equipment (and there almost certainly will be), then several kinds of microcomputers may need to be purchased. The state of current technology does not allow for a single machine that is capable of handling all possible applications of computers.

Obvious caveats to observe in choosing the equipment are: Don't buy the cheapest machine just because it is cheap. Frequently the cheapest model will be cheap because some shortcuts have been taken. Either the power of the machine will be relatively less than other machines, or the service needed for repair and troubleshooting will not be available. Also, don't buy a machine with all the options just because they are available. The appropriate analogy is found in the purchase of a new car. A buyer doesn't get all the options just because they are offered. Rather, a buyer selects those options that are going to be useful and ignores those that would only be expensive to buy and to maintain. The same should be true for computer purchases, and the decision on how the equipment is to be used will become the most important starting point in consideration of computing in the schools.

Don't buy the bottom-of-the-line model. These machines are the "come-ons" of the computer market and are designed to entice first-time buyers who have no real purpose in mind for using the equipment. In virtually all cases these machines are not powerful enough to be effective in school settings. Most educational software, for example, requires more memory than these bare-bones machines have. However, if a decision is made to approach computer literacy through programming in BASIC, then it is possible that some of these minimal machines would be a good investment. They are usually very inexpensive, and a school district could get a classroom set for little money. These machines then would have to be dedicated to the teaching of beginning programming; otherwise they might be considered only expensive toys. But the chance to be able to give lots of students lots of time with a machine is attractive.

Don't automatically buy all identical systems. Again, based on the particular decision about the uses that are to be made of the computers, it may be necessary for some of the systems to be more powerful or to have more peripheral equipment. Be sure that the machines that are bought will actually be able to do the work that needs to be done.

Fourth, in setting up a computer literacy program try to measure the hidden costs in owning the equipment. For example, how will service be provided? If the district has purchased enough equipment (and what constitutes enough depends on the kind of equipment), then it might be cost-effective to send someone from the district to a computer repair school so that service can be provided locally. If that is not feasible, then the district may want to purchase service contracts for the equipment. Another kind of hidden cost is the paper, printer tapes, disks, and other miscellaneous supplies that are needed to operate the equipment. Too, consider the costs of buying enough software for use in classes if that is one of the projected uses. And figure the costs of security for the new equipment. Finally, consider the costs of upgrading the systems as the level of skill of the students and teachers increases and as the kinds of uses for the equipment change. This particular item is frequently overlooked in figuring the cost of the initial purchase.

Fifth, an associated consideration is how much in-service will be required in order to make the program a success. In-service is expensive, in both money and time, and resource people must be available to lead the in-service programs. Someone must be in charge of the program, and that person may need released time or help from a non-teaching assistant in order to coordinate the program properly.

Sixth, where is the equipment going to be housed? In order to supply adequate security it is probably best to have a single room set aside for the computers. Then keys for the room can be limited, and access can be better monitored. However, this procedure has the disadvantage of determining a particular mode of use for the equipment; namely, whole classes are brought into the computer lab and use the machines together. This is fine for computer programming, but it is rarely the best way to use computer-assisted instructional materials. For that purpose it might be better to have machines on carts that can be moved around to the classrooms that need them. The trade-off, of course, is in providing security for those machines. Once again, the particular uses of the computers is the primary determining factor.

CAUTIONS ABOUT
COMPUTER-LITERACY
PLANNING

Two primary cautions need to be recognized by anyone who is planning a computer-literacy program. First, be sure that the local environment is well understood. Factors that need to be taken into account are the opinions and attitudes of parents, students, school board members, and local business people. Each of these groups has the potential for playing a significant role in any such program, and with their cooperation the likelihood for success is considerably greater. The role of parents, students, and school board members has already been alluded to, so it seems necessary here only to reiterate the importance of those groups. Local business people can also play a large role if they are approached carefully. Many businesses are willing to donate equipment or support for equipment. Others may be willing to provide real-world experiences, for either teachers or students, related to applications of computers. One way to begin to obtain this support is to contact businesses during the planning stages to find out what they would like school graduates to know about computers. If the school district already has established relationships with businesses through cooperative education or other intern programs, computer-literacy teachers can often tie into that existing network.

Second, be sure that the school can provide follow-up experiences for whatever program is developed. There is almost nothing more defeating for a computer-literacy program than to get students excited about the potential for computers and then not to have sufficient equipment and software available to accomplish those applications. For example, word processing holds considerable promise as a tool for improving learning, but providing enough machines for students to take advantage of this application is quite expensive. Using a word processor is effective only if each user has adequate access to the equipment. This equipment need must be considered before a school decides how many, and which, students should be taught to use a word processor. Other applications of microcomputers will also carry with them some kind of expense. These expenses should be investigated before a decision is made about which students will learn those applications.

CONCLUSION

Computer literacy is important for the remainder of this century. In spite of the differences in definitions of computer literacy, the trend now seems to be toward utilization of computing power as the central core of the idea. The trend will likely set the context for computer-literacy programs for at least the next decade.

Schools will have to invest some of their resources in developing computer-literacy programs. However, there is a lot more to starting such programs than buying equipment and telling teachers to use it. With care, schools can be successful and can satisfy the needs of teachers, students, and the community. Planning is the key.

Other
Uses of
Microcomputers

11

Microcomputers can play many supporting roles in the elementary school. These include managing students in individualized programs, maintaining grades, generating tests or worksheets, and performing administrative functions. Although the focus of this book is on instructional uses of microcomputers, the power of these machines in easing administrative burdens should not be overlooked. After administrators become convinced of the usefulness of microcomputers, it is often easier for classroom teachers to obtain the necessary institutional support for purchase of microcomputers for instructional uses.

COMPUTER-MANAGED INSTRUCTION

The use of microcomputers to maintain students' records and sequence students' activities in an objective-based program is usually referred to as computer-managed instruction (CMI). In a CMI program supported by a large computer the testing and some of the instruction may be performed directly on the computer, so the records are typically maintained automatically. On a microcomputer some of the records may have to be entered by the teacher or a teacher's aide, since there may not be enough computing power to do all of the jobs automatically.

The primary difference between CMI and CAI is that in CAI the computer administers instruction to a student, and in CMI the computer determines what the instruction is going to be. That instruction may be administered through CAI, print materials, film, tutoring, or any of many other formats. In short, a CMI system does not itself conduct instruction; it only prescribes instruction.

In CMI records are maintained in the microcomputer about the objectives that a student has mastered or the activities that have been completed. An algorithm, written by the program author, is used to determine which activity the student should work on next. If students experience difficulty with that activity, they can be cycled back through activities that will help fill in the background that may be lacking. This type of system relieves the teacher of some of the detail in remembering the status of each student and in continually making decisions about students. Too, the computer remembers every detail about every student equally well, so decisions are based on complete information stored in the computer. A teacher might, at any given time, not remember some particular detail about some particular student, and consequently the teacher's decision might not be completely appropriate. The computer's decision, on the other hand, should be appropriate.

KEEPING GRADES: AN EXAMPLE OF SPREADSHEETS

A microcomputer can easily act as an electronic gradebook, both for attendance and for maintaining grades on tests and assignments. At the end of the grading period the computer can automatically average the grades according to whatever formula or weighting system the teacher chooses. There are several gradebook programs that are very easy to learn to use, but more general spreadsheet programs, like Visicalc, could also be used for this purpose. The choice of program would depend on whether the teacher wanted the program to serve more than one specialized use.

MAIN MENU

```
 1. Adding grades
 2. List student's grades/names
 3. List class averages (& sort)
 4. List results of an activity
 5. Make class roster
 6. Make corrections (class/student)
 7. Delete grades and/or names
 8. Turn printer on/off
 9. Make letter grades (end of term)
10. Change/view grade weightings
11. Use a new class data disk
12. End
```

Figure 11.1 Primary options

From Apple, *Gradebook Manual*, page 3.

One example of a gradebook program is Apple Gradebook. This program provides several standard options for keeping grades (Figure 11.1). Options 6, 7, and 9, in turn, each have several suboptions (Figure 11.2). Each function that the program allows puts its own prompts on the screen, so a computer-literate teacher can learn to use this program in relatively few minutes.

The use of multiple menus to present different sets of functions is very common in utility programs like gradebooks or word processors. The menus allow the programmer to present all the relevant information a user needs at any given moment, and they allow the screen to be kept uncluttered. The user then does not have to refer constantly to a reference manual, so use of the program is easier and more efficient.

A gradebook is one example of a use of a more general utility program called a spreadsheet program. A spreadsheet allows a user to make projections or to do calculations based on potentially changing data. Spreadsheets were originally designed for business applications, but they do have some applications in the classroom. They can help students learn to plan ahead and to ask appropriate questions. Spreadsheets allow users to predict how the world might be under hypothetical conditions; the key in using them effectively is to be able to

CORRECTION MODULE

This module is entered by choosing option 6 (Make corrections), in the main menu. When you first enter this module, you are given the following choices:
1. Add a new student.
2. Delete a student.
3. Change a grade.
4. Correct spelling of a name.
5. Add a new class.
6. Return to main grade book menu.

DELETION MODULE

As stated previously, this option is used to delete classes, a set of student's grades, or all students' grades. When you choose this module from the main grade book menu, the following will appear on the screen:
1. Delete all grades, and student's names. Enables you to start with new classes.
2. Delete grades of students only. Used for a new term with the same students.
3. Delete only one class.
4. Delete one set of grades.
5. Return to main grade book menu.
6. Quit

END OF TERM MODULE

With this option you can obtain a histogram of student's grades and convert student class averages to letter grades. When you choose this option from the main menu, the following new menu will appear on the screen:
1. View student averages (ranked by grades).
2. View histogram of student averages.
3. Convert student averages to letter grades.
4. Turn printer on/off.
5. Return to main menu.

Figure 11.2   Suboptions

From Apple, *Gradebook Manual*, pages 7–10.

structure the range of hypotheses so that the predictions are meaningful.

For example, a spreadsheet might be used to plan a school party by projecting costs and needs for various combinations of younger and older students. They can also be used to ask "what if" questions. How long would it take to save a million bottle caps if every student collected five bottle caps per day? If grades 1–3 students collected two bottle caps per day and grades 4–6 students collected six bottle caps per day? If students only collected bottle caps on the weekends?

Although there is much potential in using spreadsheets, the advantage for learning is only beginning to be investigated. Much more experience in classroom use is needed. In particular, because use of spreadsheets involves some symbol manipulation skill, how can elementary students be best introduced to spreadsheets? It was not until about late 1985 that simplified versions of spreadsheets, suitable for use in elementary schools, were introduced commercially. Teachers need now to get copies of these programs and try them out with students in their classes.

CREATING TESTS AND WORKSHEETS: AN EXAMPLE OF DATA BASES

Microcomputers are very good at remembering information accurately and completely. One type of application of this capability is in maintaining a bank of test items. As good items are developed over the course of several years, they can be saved on disk. When enough items for particular content have been saved, multiple forms of a test can be created by randomly selecting items that test that content. In this way, students can each receive different forms of a test, or a single student can be given the option of multiple testing, with different tests covering the same content. This is particularly important in a mastery learning situation when it is essential that multiple testing be allowed.

Some commercial programs that are now being developed and published provide the items for particular content, but teachers can also begin to develop their own item banks, either individually or collectively. Items can be tested with students and altered as needed, and they can be modified at any time to adjust to changes in the curriculum or in the backgrounds of the students. For example, an item bank on computer literacy in 1985 would probably need considerable alteration by 1990, just because the computer experiences that the students will bring to school by that time will be much different.

Brown (1982) described one locally developed test bank, run on a minicomputer, for junior and senior high schools. It contains over 64,000 objective test items, selected from more than 300,000 and classified by Library of Congress codes. A user can request a test of a specific number of items on a given topic or topics, and the test will be printed out. Students can also access the test bank through a quiz routine for purposes of study, drill, or just enjoyment.

Multiple forms of worksheets on a given topic could also be produced from item banks. The exercises could be randomly selected and printed out. A ditto master could be made from that copy, or multiple copies could be printed out directly by the computer.

A slightly different approach is for the teacher to enter a set of exercises into a worksheet-generation program and then have the computer randomly order the items to produce a different version for each student. This requires more time from the teacher each time the worksheets are made, but it saves the time needed to maintain the item bank. If worksheets are going to be only infrequently generated by computer, this might be the better way to proceed. Too, it is slightly more flexible in terms of the particular exercises to be included on the worksheet.

Computer programs for generating crossword (or crossnumber) puzzles and for word-search puzzles are also available. These programs accept the words and definitions, or just the words for the word-search puzzle, and then arrange them in a predetermined crossword template or in a grid of letters. For example, the following word-search grid was generated by a computer program. The program prints the grid, and it also prints a key to use if desired (Figure 11.3).

Test-generation programs are examples of a more general type of program, called a data base program. A data base acts like an elec-

```
. . . . . . T . . . . . . . .
. . . . . . R . . . . . . .
. . . . . . . A . . . . . .
. . . . S . . E . . E . .
. B . . . L . . . H U . . .
. R . . . . I . . G . . .
. A . . . . S N . . . H .
. I . . . . O N . . T . .
. N . . . T . . O E . . .
. . . . . . . . . E T . . L
Y R A L L I P A C T . . . U L
Y E N D I K V S P L E E N I .
. . . . E . . E . . . G V . .
. . . Y . . . . I . S E . . .
. . E . . . . . N R . . . .
```

BODY PARTS

```
Q Y R S L H T F X O H O D N V
M E R V L V M R C J W D S Y Z
F P D B E M S U A Y Z J X A Q
S A Z X O S P R X E G L E W O
D B Q F B O L O V I H U Q B R
O R J O C X J I I V G K P P Y
M A O Z Y R N B S N G P S H E
N I J N F A X K O N D Q T Q W
O N O P Y X R T L I O E T O D
X C K A S R U U H G E T C O L
Y R A L L I P A C T R I T U L
Y E N D I K V S P L E E N I V
T R R J E H W E F O G G V X J
D X A Y N R S C I X S E N W K
O A E D U W B Y I N R Q G J F
```

THERE ARE 12 WORDS HERE - CAN YOU FIND THEM?

HERE ARE THE ONES TO LOOK FOR

BRAIN	CAPILLARY	EYE
HEART	KIDNEY	LIVER
LUNGS	SPLEEN	TEETH
TONGUE	TONSILS	VEIN

Figure 11.3 Word Search Grid

tronic card file, with the computer being able to search for any information requested by the user. Students can create their own data
bases of interest; for example, personal favorite items like movies, TV
shows, sports teams, etc. Searching can then be done and students
can make summaries of the information found by the computer.
Organizing and creating graphs of these summaries becomes a natural
classroom activity. In a unit on world geography a data base could
be made of information on countries; for example, land area, population, type of government, major industries, major exports. Students
then could ask the computer to find all countries that have fewer than
fifty million people or that export oil.

    Educators at all levels are just beginning to imagine how to help
students deal with vast quantities of information. Learning to use data
bases by asking the right questions at the right time will undoubtedly
be an important part of coping with this information. We need much
more experience, however, in knowing how to provide appropriate
help to students in this process.

NETWORKING

Networking is one of the computer uses that is still relatively far away
for most schools. Networking means having computers connected to
each other, either in a local setting (e.g., a computer lab) or in long-
distance settings (e.g., over telephone lines). Information can then be
shared among the connected computers so that users can talk directly
to each other through their computer screens.

    The problem for schools in implementing networks seems to be
in having enough hardware to dedicate to the network, for networked
computers are less easily transportable. Networks are beginning to
appear, however, both in large urban school districts and in single
buildings. The chore now is to learn how to use the networks to
enhance learning.

    The primary advantage of using a network would seem to be the
ability to communicate with all users at all times. Students can very
easily get help from each other as well as from the teacher in a network
environment. Research on peer teaching may provide some insight on

how to proceed in using networking to improve learning. However, teachers should refrain from rushing too quickly into this relatively sophisticated application of computer capabilities. Just because networking can be done does not mean it will be a useful technique for every school.

CONCLUSION

Many teaching chores can be made easier through use of computer tools. The time saved might be spent by the teacher in providing more individual attention to students, thus making the classroom environment more personal. Simultaneously, teachers will learn to use computing power in their everyday professional lives. The attitudes that they develop about the uses and misuses of computers will provide valuable material for their teaching of attitudes to students. Teachers who are comfortable with computers are more likely to have students who are similarly comfortable with computers. Comfort with computers is one of the most important legacies for today's students.

References

Alberta Education. (1983). *Computer courseware evaluations, January 1983 to May 1985*. Edmonton, Alberta, Canada: the author.

Anderson, J. J. (1983, June). Bank Street Writer: A review. *Creative Computing, 9*(6), 33–34.

Anderson, R. E., and Klassen, D. L. (1981). A conceptual framework for developing computer literacy instruction. *AEDS Journal, 14*, 128–150.

Apple Computer. (1979). *Lemonade Stand* (software). Cupertino, CA: the author.

Ashlock, R. B. (1972). *Error patterns in computation*. Columbus, OH: Charles E. Merrill.

Ashlock, R. B., and Humphrey, J. H. (1976). *Teaching elementary school mathematics through motor learning*. Springfield, IL: Charles C. Thomas.

Barclay, T. (1982). "BUGGY": Outfitting for the great error hunt. *Classroom Computer News, 2*(4), 25, 27.

Behr, M. J.; Lesh, R.; Post, T. R.; and Silver, E. (1982). Rational number concepts. In R. Lesh and M. Landau, eds., *Acquisition of mathematical concepts and processes*, pp. 91–126. New York, NY: Academic Press.

Bell, F. H. (1982). Implementing instructional computing and computer literacy in a school or college. *AEDS Journal, 15*, 169–176.

Birnbaum, J. S. (1985). Toward the domestication of computers. In J. F. Traub, ed., *Cohabiting with computers*. Los Altos, CA: William Kaufman, Inc.

Bitter, G. (1982). The road to computer literacy: A scope and sequence model. *Electronic Learning, 2*(1), 60–63.

Bloom, B. S., ed. (1956). *Taxonomy of educational objectives*. New York, NY: McKay.

Blume, G. W. (1984, April). *A review of research on the effects of computer programming on mathematical problem solving*. Paper presented at the annual meeting of the American Educational Research Association, New Orleans, LA.

Bork, A. (1981). *Learning with computers*. Bedford, MA: Digital Equipment Corporation.

Bork, A. (1983). Two examples of computer-based learning on personal computers. *AEDS Journal, 17*(1 & 2), 49–53.

Bowen, J. J. (1970). The use of games as an instructional media. Doctoral dissertation,

University of California, Los Angeles, 1969. *Dissertation Abstracts International, 30*, 3358A–3359A. (University Microfilms No. 70–2189).

Bracey, G. W. (1982). Computers in education: What the research shows. *Electronic Learning, 2*(3), 51–54.

Bright, G. W. (1983). Explaining the efficiency of computer-assisted instruction. *AEDS Journal, 16*, 144–152.

Bright, G. W. (1984a). Computer diagnosis of errors. *School Science and Mathematics, 84*, 208–219.

Bright, G. W. (1984b). Real-time diagnosis of computation errors in drill and practice CAI. In H. N. Cheek, J. M. Hill, and G. W. Bright, eds., *Diagnostic and prescriptive mathematics: Issues, ideas, and insights: 1984 RCDPM research monograph,* pp. 44–52. Kent, OH: Research Council for Diagnostic and Prescriptive Mathematics.

Bright, G. W.; Harvey, J. G.; and Wheeler, M. M. (1979a). Using games to retrain skills with basic multiplication facts. *Journal for Research in Mathematics Education, 10*, 103–110.

Bright, G. W.; Harvey, J. G.; and Wheeler, M. M. (1979b). Incorporating instructional objectives into the rules of a game. *Journal for Research in Mathematics Education, 10*, 356–359.

Bright, G. W.; Harvey, J. G.; and Wheeler, M. M. (1980a). Achievement grouping with mathematics concept and skill games. *Journal of Educational Research, 73*, 265–269.

Bright, G. W.; Harvey, J. G.; and Wheeler, M. M. (1980b). Using games to maintain multiplication basic facts. *Journal for Research in Mathematics Education, 11*, 379–385.

Bright, G. W.; Harvey, J. G.; and Wheeler, M. M. (1980c). Game constraints, player verbalizations, and mathematics learning. *Journal of Experimental Education, 49*, 52–55.

Bright, G. W.; Harvey, J. G.; and Wheeler, M. M. (1981). Varying manipulative game constraints. *Journal of Educational Research, 74*, 347–351.

Bright, G. W.; Harvey, J. G.; and Wheeler, M. M. (1983). Use of a game to instruct on logical reasoning. *School Science and Mathematics, 83*, 396–405.

Bright, G. W.; Harvey, J. G.; and Wheeler, M. M. (1985). *Learning and mathematics games. Journal for Research in Mathematics Education,* Monograph Number 1. Reston, VA: National Council of Teachers of Mathematics.

Brown, B. (1982). Automated test and quiz production. *Classroom Computer News, 2*(4), 33,35.

Brown, J. S., and Burton, R. R. (1978). Diagnostic models for procedural bugs in basic mathematical skills. *Cognitive Science, 2*, 155–192.

Brown, S. W., and Rood, M. K. (1984, April). *Training gifted students in LOGO and BASIC: What is the difference?* Paper presented at the annual meeting of the American Educational Research Association, New Orleans, LA.

Brownell, W. A. (1935). Psychological considerations in the learning and the teaching of arithmetic. In *The teaching of arithmetic: Tenth NCTM yearbook,* pp. 1–31. Washington, DC: National Council of Teachers of Mathematics.

Doctoral dissertation, Saint Louis University, 1978. *Dissertation Abstracts International*, *39*, 6008A. (University Microfilms No. 7908313)

Wheeler, L. R., and Wheeler, V. D. (1940). An experimental study in learning to read numerals. *Mathematics Teacher*, *33*, 25–31.

Woerner, K. L. W. (1980). Computer based diagnosis and remediation of computational errors with fractions. Doctoral dissertation, The University of Texas at Austin, 1980. *Dissertation Abstracts International*, *41*, 1455A. (University Microfilms No. 8021529)

Wolff, D. J. (1974). An instructional game program: Its effect on task motivation. Doctoral dissertation, Rutgers University, 1974. *Dissertation Abstracts International*, *35*, 3535A–3536A. (University Microfilms, No. 74–27,352)

Wynroth, L. Z. (1970). Learning arithmetic by playing games. Doctoral dissertation, Cornell University, 1970. *Dissertation Abstracts International*, *31*, 942A–943A. (University Microfilms No. 70–14,410)

Index

Brownell, W. A. (1947). The place of meaning in the teaching of arithmetic. *Elementary School Journal, 47*, 256–265.

Chaffee, M. R. (1982). Viewpoint: Use of microcomputers in the elementary and junior high schools. *Classroom Computer News, 2*(4), 17,76.

Champagne, A. B., and Rogalska-Saz, J. (1984). In V. P. Hansen and M. J. Zweng, eds., *Computers in mathematics education: 1984 NCTM yearbook*, pp. 43–53. Reston, VA: National Council of Teachers of Mathematics.

Clements, D. H., and Gullo, D. F. (1984, April). *Effects of computer programming on young children's cognition*. Paper presented at the annual meeting of the National Council of Teachers of Mathematics.

Cody, R. (1973). Computers in education: A review. *Journal of College Science Teaching, 3*, 22–28.

Cupertino Union School District. (1983). K–8 computer literacy curriculum: Revised 1982. *Computing Teacher, 10*(7), 7–10.

Daiute, C. (1982). Word processing: Can it make even good writers better? *Electronic Learning, 1*(4), 29–31.

Dennis, R. J.; Muiznieks, V. J.; and Stewart, J. T. (1979). *Instructional games and the computer-using teacher*. Urbana, IL: Department of Secondary Education, University of Illinois. (ERIC Document Reproduction Service No. ED 183 189)

Department of Defense Dependents Schools. (1982, January). *Educational Computing*. Washington, DC: the author.

Deringer, D. K., and Molnar, A. R. (1982). Key components for a national computer literacy program. In R. J. Seidel, R. E. Anderson, and B. Hunter, eds., *Computer literacy: Issues and directions for 1985*. New York, NY: Academic Press.

Digest of Educational Software Reviews: Education. (1984). *Ernie's Quiz*. Fresno, CA: the author.

Droter, R. (1972). *A comparison of active games and passive games used as learning media for the development of arithmetic readiness skills and concepts with kindergarten children in an attempt to study gross motor activity as a learning facilitator*. Unpublished doctoral dissertation, University of Maryland, College Park, MD.

Edwards, J.; Norton, S.; Taylor, S.; Weiss, M.; and Van Dusseldorp, R. (1975). How effective is CAI - A review of the research. *Educational Leadership, 33*, 147–153.

Fishell, F. E. (1975). The effect of a math trading game on achievement and attitude in fifth grade division. Doctoral dissertation, Michigan State University, 1975. *Dissertation Abstracts International, 36*, 3382A. (University Microfilms No. 75–27,262)

Fisher, G. (1984). The social effects of computers in education. *Electronic Learning, 3*(6), 26,28.

Ginsburg, H. P. (in press). Academic diagnosis: Contributions from developmental psychology. In J. Valsiner, ed., *The role of the individual subject in scientific psychology*. New York: Plenum.

Ginsburg, H. P., and Allardice, B. S. (1984). Children's difficulties with school mathematics. In B. Rogoff and J. Lave, eds., *Everyday cognition: Its development in social context*, pp. 194–219. Cambridge, MA: Harvard University Press.

Goldberg, S. (1980). The effects of the use of strategy games on the problem solving ability of selected seventh grade students. Doctoral dissertation, Temple University, 1980. *Dissertation Abstracts International, 41*, 1990A. (University Microfilms No. 80–25082)

Henney, M. (1983). The effect of all-capital vs. regular mixed print, as presented on a computer screen, on reading rate and accuracy. *AEDS Journal, 16*, 205–217.

Hoover, J. H. (1921). Motivated drill work in third-grade arithmetic and silent reading. *Journal of Educational Research, 4*, 200–211.

Hopkins, M. H. (1978). The diagnosis of learning styles in arithmetic. *Arithmetic Teacher, 25*(7), 47–50.

Humphrey, J. H. (1966). An exploratory study of active games in learning of number concepts by first-grade boys and girls. *Perceptual and Motor Skills, 23*, 341–342.

Hunter, B. (1982). Computer literacy curriculum for grades K–8. In R. J. Seidel, R. E. Anderson, and B. Hunter, eds., *Computer literacy: Issues and directions for 1985*. New York, NY: Academic Press.

Jamison, D.; Suppes, P.; and Wells, S. (1974). The effectiveness of alternative instructional media: A survey. *Review of Educational Research, 44*, 1–67.

Jensen, C. B. (1982). The enhanced CAI tutorial, In *Proceedings of the National Educational Computing Conference*, Kansas City, KS: National Educational Computing Conference.

Kansky, R.; Heck, W.; and Johnson, J. (1981). *Guidelines for evaluating computerized instructional materials*. Reston, VA: National Council of Teachers of Mathematics.

Karlin, M. W. (1972). The development and utilization of a card game for teaching prime factorization in the fifth grade. Doctoral dissertation, University of Colorado, 1971. *Dissertation Abstracts International, 33*, 80A. (University Microfilms No. 72–17,272)

Kayser, R., and King, G. (1984). 7 steps to buying software. *Electronic Education, 6*(3), 14,56.

Knapp, L. (1984). Word processors. *Electronic Learning, 3*(6), 54–56.

Kraus, W. H. (1981). Using a computer game to reinforce skills in addition basic facts in second grade. *Journal for Research in Mathematics Education, 12*, 152–155.

Kraus, W. H. (1982a). *Fish Chase* (software). St. Louis, MO: Milliken Educational Publishers.

Kraus, W. H. (1982b). *Golf Classic* (software). St. Louis, MO: Milliken Educational Publishers.

Kraus, W. H. (1982c). *Jar Game* (software). St. Louis, MO: Milliken Educational Publishers.

Kulik, J. A.; Kulik, C. C.; and Cohen, P. A. (1980). Effectiveness of computer-based college teaching: A meta-analysis of the findings. *Review of Educational Research, 50*, 525–544.

Lesh, R. A., Jr., and Johnson, H. C. (1976). Models and applications as advanced organizers. *Journal for Research in Mathematics Education, 7*, 75–81.

Lewis, C., and Mack, R. (1982). Learning to use a text processing system: Evidence from "thinking aloud" protocols. In *Human factors in computer systems*. Washington, DC: National Bureau of Standards.

Luehrmann, A. (1981). Computer literacy: What should it be? *Mathematics Teacher*, 74, 682–686.

Luster, R. G. (1983). *Four-Letter Words* (software). Iowa City, IA: Conduit.

Malone, T. (1980, August). *What makes things fun to learn? A study of intrinsically motivating computer games* (Report CIS–7, SSL–80–11). Palo Alto, CA: Xerox Palo Alto Research Center.

Mayer, R. E. (1982). Contributions of cognitive science and related research in learning to the design of computer literacy curricula. In R. J. Seidel, R. E. Anderson, and B. Hunter, eds., *Computer literacy: Issues and directions for 1985*, pp. 129–159. New York: Academic Press.

Minnesota Educational Computing Consortium. (1980a). *A guide to developing instructional software for the Apple II microcomputer* (MECC publication #M(AP) - 2). St. Paul, MN: the author.

Minnesota Educational Computer Consortium. (1980b). *Elementary volume 3* (software and print materials). St. Paul, MN: the author.

Minnesota Educational Computer Consortium. (1980c). *Elementary volume 4* (software and print materials). St. Paul, MN: the author.

Minnesota Educational Computing Consortium. (1980d). *Elementary volume 5* (software and print materials). St. Paul, MN: the author.

Minnesota Educational Computing Consortium. (1980e). *Elementary volume 9* (software and print materials). St. Paul, MN: the author.

Minnesota Educational Computing Consortium. (1980f). *Science volume 3* (software and print materials). St. Paul, MN: the author.

Minnesota Educational Computing Consortium. (1980g). *Social studies volume 2* (software and print materials). St. Paul, MN: the author.

Minnesota Educational Computing Consortium. (1983a). *Early addition* (software and print materials). St. Paul, MN: the author.

Minnesota Educational Computer Consortium. (1983b). *Oh, Deer!* (software and print materials). St. Paul, MN: the author.

Mitzel, H. E. (1981). On the importance of theory in applying technology to education. *Journal of Computer-Based Instruction*, 7, 93–98.

National Council of Teachers of Mathematics. (1980). *An agenda for action: School mathematics in the 1980s*. Reston, VA: the author.

O'Brien, T. C. (1982). *Teasers by Tobbs* (software). Pleasantville, NY: Sunburst Communications.

Overton, V. (1981). Research in instructional computing and mathematics education. *Viewpoints in Teaching and Learning*, 57(2), 23–26.

Papert, S. (1980). *Mindstorms: Children, computers, and powerful ideas*. New York: Basic Books.

Peele, H. A. (1972). A study of computer-assisted learning with artificial intelligence games. Doctoral dissertation, University of Massachusetts, 1971. *Dissertation Abstracts International*, 32, 6690A. (University Microfilms No. 72–18,259)

Piper, K. (1984). Word processing as a tool for structured writing instruction with elementary students. *AEDS Monitor*, 23(1 & 2), 22–24.

Polya, G. (1973). *How to solve it* (2d ed.). Princeton, NJ: Princeton University Press.

Rampy, L. M. (1984, April). *The problem-solving style of fifth graders using Logo*.

Paper presented at the annual meeting of the American Educational Research Association, New Orleans, LA.

Reiser, R. A., and Gerlach, V. S. (1976, April). *Research on simulation games in education: A critical analysis.* Paper presented at the annual meeting of the American Educational Research Association, San Francisco, CA.

Resources in Computer Education. (undated). *Sample review printout.* Portland, OR: the author.

Riel, M. (1985). The computer chronicles newswire: A functional learning environment for acquiring literacy skills. *Journal of Educational Computing Research,* *1,* 317–337.

Roblyer, M. D. (1981). Instructional design versus authoring of courseware: Some crucial differences. *AEDS Journal, 14,* 173–181.

Ross, D. (1970). Incidental learning of number concepts in small group games. *American Journal of Mental Deficiency, 74,* 718–725.

School Microware Review. (1981). *Review form.* Dresden, ME: the author.

Sharples, M. (1983). The use of computers to aid the teaching of creative writing. *AEDS Journal, 16,* 79–91.

Shumway, R. J. (1984). Young children, programming, and mathematical thinking. In V. P. Hansen and M. J. Zweng, eds., *Computers in mathematics education: 1984 NCTM Yearbook,* pp. 127–134. Reston, VA: National Council of Teachers of Mathematics.

Slattow, G. (1977, March). *Demonstration of the PLATO IV computer-based education system.* Urbana, IL: University of Illinois Computer-based Educational Research Laboratory. (ERIC Document Reproduction System No. ED 158 767)

Soloway, E.; Lochhead, J.; and Clement, J. (1982). Does computer programming enhance problem solving ability? Some positive evidence on algebra word problems. In R. J. Seidel, R. E. Anderson, and B. Hunter, eds., *Computer literacy: Issues and directions for 1985,* pp. 171–185. New York: Academic Press.

Sovchik, R., and Heddens, J. W. (1978). Classroom diagnosis and remediation. *Arithmetic Teacher, 25*(4), 47–49.

Steinway, L. S. (1918). An experiment in games involving a knowledge of number. *Teachers College Record, 19,* 43–53.

Thomas, D. B. (1979). The effectiveness of computer assisted instruction in secondary schools. *AEDS Journal, 12,* 103–116.

Travis, B. P. (1978). The diagnosis and remediation of learning difficulties of community college developmental mathematics students using computer technology. Doctoral dissertation, The University of Texas at Austin, 1978. *Dissertation Abstracts International, 39,* 2115A. (University Microfilms No. 7817722)

Travis, B. P. (1984). Computer diagnosis of algorithmic errors. In V. P. Hansen and M. J. Zweng, eds., *Computers in mathematics education: 1984 NCTM yearbook,* pp. 211–216. Reston, VA: National Council of Teachers of Mathematics.

Travis, B. P., and Carry, L. R. (1983). Computer diagnosis and remediation strategies for algorithmic errors. *Focus on Learning Problems in Mathematics, 5*(3 & 4), 35–45.

Trimmer, R. G. (1979). A study of logical reasoning using the game Master Mind.